Le Corbusier   Creation is a Patient Search

LE CORBUSIER

CREATION IS A PATIENT SEARCH

Translated by James Palmes

Introduction by Maurice Jardot

Frederick A. Praeger, Publishers, New York · Washington

BOOKS THAT MATTER

Published in the United States of America in 1960
by Frederick A. Praeger, Inc., Publishers
111 Fourth Avenue, New York, N. Y. 10003
Third printing, 1967
All rights reserved
© Le Corbusier, 1960
Library of Congress Catalog Card Number: 60-53113
Printed in Germany

CONTENTS

INTRODUCTION

SKETCH FOR A PORTRAIT

It often happens that, in a reformer, the man is obscured by the teacher and that the attitudes which circumstances demand are taken for qualities of character: his actions both expose and hide their author, and the picture painted by his renown is more of a mask than a mirror. Nobody in our day has had more to endure than Le Corbusier from the misrepresentations which fame bestows. That is why this "sketch for a portrait" may be of some use in prefacing a book containing the essence of a life-work, upon which an ill-informed, wayward and insensitive opinion has based its conception of the man who composed it.

In his desire to redress the balance, the writer of these lines is laying himself open to a charge of presumption. For, to be frank, he has no more right than others to sustain this rôle. And yet, if he is not the sole, nor the oldest, nor the closest, friend of Le Corbusier, he is perhaps less burdened than most by those innumerable interests which batten on friendship or which are often its principal inspiration. He is neither an architect, nor a pupil, nor a collaborator, nor a client, nor the holder of the least particle of authority in the world of building, and he believes that this absence of entitlement is here an advantage. He is in fact merely someone who would like to speak in the simplest possible terms of another man, exceptional, famous and misunderstood, who one day did him the supreme and never to be forgotten honour of responding by friendship to his eager, and affectionate, admiration.

He does not have the open expression and the easy smile of those who readily inspire sympathy; animation and grace are lacking; the eyes are dull, the voice is flat and uneven. But candour and strength reinforce an impressive demeanour seemingly built for defence, behind which he appears to withdraw, to watch and to observe. It is very hard not to feel respect and curiosity!

He has known (and still knows) incomprehension, hostility, betrayal and, worse still, gross injustice. For more than forty years he has had to wage war – on his own ground of architecture and planning – against the entrenched forces of academic thinking, to draw up an inventory of what is essential and possible, and then to stir into activity imaginations long tethered to weary insensibility. He has roused and shaken, he has condemned and disturbed, and such things are not easy to forgive! – Honour and success have admittedly not been denied him, but his real victory, which for some time now has been swaying French opinion and leaving its mark upon the best new buildings of the country, a victory unobtrusive, but broad and decisive, has been stolen from him by those who continually and brazenly wear his mantle as their own. He is revered, but brushed aside, and it almost always seems that the principles and solutions which he has elaborated are assigned for others to put into practice. Hence the porcupine manner with which he is sometimes reproached. But how can we expect a more engaging, a more sympathetic presence, in one who knows that he owes the principal difficulties of his life as an artist to those rare qualities which are peculiarly his? Although the circumstances in which he works link the architect-planner much more closely than the painter to his social environment, since it provides the former with the legitimate expectation of commissions, which the latter can more easily do without, it is none the less of Cézanne whom one thinks when faced with certain characteristics of Le Corbusier. There is the same expostulating abruptness, the same churlishness proclaiming more than it hides the quick resentments of easily ruffled sensibility, and all of this grafted on to an obstinate, patient, exemplary firmness of character; in each of them, a pride usually subdued, a humility sure of itself and the conviction, uneasily, but strongly, held (and so often justified) of being a leader among his peers; the same way, too, of giving and withdrawing, of seeking and evading contact, the constant fear in short of finding himself too closely involved, yet always actuated by a stubborn desire simply to occupy an undisputed place of his own. Even the habit of drowning thoughts in a torrent of words, of deliberately misinterpreting a question considered too direct and tactless, can be found in both; cuttle-fish eject ink; these two, in moments of crisis, spread a dense verbal fog. And this manner of standing apart – a lone wolf –, which one finds without surprise in Cézanne, how has it been able to survive in Le Corbusier the enthusiasm of his pupils, the affection of his friends, the immensity of his fame and all those links with the world which his work in planning and architecture have created? The answer seems to lie in that region of Aix and Marseille, where their two destinies have converged, and where their genius has also been honoured by the mockery of fools.

A singular person, whose outlines fall into a more intelligible pattern when we are familiar with the particular mirrors in which we should normally expect to find his reflection. For some years Le Corbusier can really only be seen as Don Quixote, Gargantua and Pantagruel, and occasionally as Ulysses. In imagination his library might well be confined to the works of Homer, Cervantes and Rabelais, supplemented, however, by the more serious and recent studies of the "Catharic Heresy", all the more significant because of its widespread acceptance in that district of France in which Le Corbusier, not without reason, has set the cradle of his family. Every facet of his mind, every instinct of his temperament is there: the vivid invention, the novel, unpredictable, poetic language, the mystic visionary fervour, the logical precision, the abounding sensuousness, the lofty moral principles, the loneliness and the strength of purpose. And everywhere, and above everything, a certain view of mankind, a vast all-embracing view in which there is a constant epic quality. For it is at this level, in an exuberance of ideas and opinions that Le Corbusier finds his natural place. Here, and from a distance, he can take stock of all the things there are to love, to judge and to reform. Here he can perfect, day in day out, with the help of more and more products of his unending researches, the most elaborate and original conception that any architect-planner of our generation has had of the things which concern his profession. What in fact constitutes the fundamental uniqueness of Le Corbusier's work and which shines forth so brilliantly is that the technical demands of structure, programme and aesthetics are felt to be parts of a far wider vision in which the whole "field of building" becomes in the final analysis the chosen setting of human relations, which it is man's duty to-day to re-establish and maintain with nature, on the one hand, and with his fellows, on the other. There is something staggering in this will to create a new harmonious environment, when, as goes without saying, so little can be done whilst men cling to the structural forms of other days; in this noble ambition, based upon the longing for security and the need for freedom, in which our age can see reflected some of the dreams which it is occupied so clumsily and painfully in realizing. With respect to the professor at the École des Hautes Études who seems to be confusing orderliness with regimentation, there is a way of taking other people into consideration without abandoning one's principles, for there are "restraints" which serve the interests of freedom, like those, for instance, reserving pavements for pedestrians and roads for cars; and it is these, and these alone, which Le Corbusier commends to our attention.

This, or something like it, is Le Corbusier at work; the man who meets and receives his friends in the normal contacts of everyday life cannot obviously be a complete stranger to the other, but he could fall a little below his standard. In fact "Corbu" remains no less worthy of Le Corbusier when he is not standing on ceremony.
Those who do know him, or do not know him well, often talk of his difficult character, aggressiveness, egoism,

complacency and especially of a somewhat bleak attitude of mind making no allowances for doubts and shades of opinion. This, however, is no more than an ungracious front turned to the enemy, to keep him at arm's length, for there must be no yielding to the blandishments of compromise. The "Corbu" of his friends is quite different: argumentative and ironical, at times, certainly; but exquisitely kind and perceptive, although sometimes concealing this behind a rather gruff exterior; the modesty of his behaviour, the respect which he shows to the views and opinions of others, and the attention which he gives them, are always exemplary when he is with people who, he knows, appreciate and like him. But he can become contemptuous and harsh, it is true, in front of cowards, opportunists and time-servers, and towards all those who care nothing for the profession which they have had the privilege to choose for themselves. Because they bring dishonour to what he feels it to be so great an honour to serve, he naturally reserves his wrath for the great mass of architects who have neither knowledge, talent nor enthusiasm, for the rabble of practitioners, without conscience or intelligence, by whom architecture was for so long threatened with extinction. His friends consider him uncommonly generous and unselfish, but he can be scathingly unkind to those whom, rightly or wrongly, he suspects of wanting to take a mean advantage of his indifference to so-called material benefits. He wavers little, if at all, in the face of injustice or slights, but he is suddenly disarmed and reduced to tears by an unexpected show of affection, respect, attachment or devotion. According to his own account, he begins every new day by comparing himself with the least of mortals, by the inexorable process of listing in his mind the qualities and aptitudes which he lacks. To this salutary examination, which no doubt occurs less frequently than he says, may well be due the acute sense of incompetence which Le Corbusier feels in approaching matters outside his particular experience, and his stubborn refusal to be drawn on to ground with which he is not completely familiar. And to all this we must add that his honour, if hypersensitive, is beyond question and his rectitude inflexible, while his actions, although occasionally maladroit, are never guided by deception or intrigue.

And he loves good food and good stories.

"Ontogenesis reproduces phylogenesis!" We still recall the metaphysical flutter which we experienced in our philosophy class on first hearing this axiom, according to which the development of the individual reflects that of the species: it seemed at once luminous and impenetrably obscure. It is a light, a dark profundity, a stimulus not unlike this which Le Corbusier seems to be seeking in history, in those supreme moments which inspired migrations, invasions, annexations and revolutions, and multiplied discoveries; in those times of great movements of commerce, thought, manners and religion; in short, in everything which leaves traces and implies continuity, and without which mankind and the world would not be what they are to-day. The vast panoramas of history enchant him, and it was perhaps to enable us to share his pleasure that he conceived the "museum of knowledge", where we shall be able to absorb and follow step by step the multifarious history of our painful, but marvellous, evolution. The past exists first and foremost to justify and illuminate the present, but also to supply us from this source and that with the features which have, as it were, spontaneously combined to-day to draw the picture of our world and the portrait of ourselves. Of course Le Corbusier does not expect from us that we should relive the history of mankind as the foetus remoulds to its purposes the biogenetic evolution of the species; nor from architecture that it should repeat in our day the various stages of its development. For him, none the less, there is a strong and fundamental bond between the present and the past, which is not established by our heritage, still less by a taste for imitation, but one created by the possibility and the duty to accept as close and almost tangible what has gone before. This sense of obligation to the past is a marked feature of our age – which, as we know, has manifested the most lively and praiseworthy interest in prehistory and early civilizations, and at the same time a horrible partiality for the more artificial versions of the simple life – but nobody feels it more instinctively and deeply than Le Corbusier. For this protagonist of the "machine civilization", and of industrial technology, this very early admirer – before 1920 – of the subtle audacities of cubism, who was among the first to recognize the aesthetic merits of mass-produced articles (his "purist" pictures are before all else the ultimate expression of the essential, undramatic, beauty of "standards") was also the man who was touched by the simplicity of André Bauchant, a painter whom he helped to make known, and who does not hesitate, when the occasion demands, to use a rough and ready building material like pisé (Murondins Houses 1940), to take lessons in proportions and dignity from an old country cottage, or to gather up with delighted surprise, from the beach or the lane, some specimen of "natural art", be it leaf or bone, root or pebble, flint or shell. Such is his all-embracing outlook. It rejects nothing, or very little.

As for man, to him he is always and everywhere the same, whether he comes from Neanderthal or is Einstein himself! – And of the nobility which Le Corbusier never grudges him, he can even discover traces as clearly, or nearly so, in the mechanics of our bodies as in the workings of our minds.

An attitude like this is impossible without his supremely simple sense of moral values. How difficult it is to leave out the "man of principle" when speaking of Le Corbusier!

Any parade of wealth, power or importance he finds offensive and vulgar. Radically opposed to the big-business approach common among architects and planners to-day, this truly great man has never sought the favour of influential clients. Comfortably established and occupied as few men are, he remains serene and undisturbed among the telephones, secretaries, dictaphones and typists, which to many are the outward signs of authority. To an increasing extent indeed, everything about him seems to conform to a scale and pattern which a man may reasonably find convenient. Both as the craftsman, for which he was apprenticed at La Chaux-de-Fond, and as the artist, which he becomes so completely when he paints, what matters to Le Corbusier in his work is the fundamental process of creation, which can really only be effective when one has guided it oneself from hesitant beginnings to final realization. That is why No. 35 rue de Sèvres is to-day only the place where plans and models are made. The organization of the job and its technical supervision on the site are entrusted – but not left – to specialist firms, a division of labour illustrating, incidentally, Le Corbusier's conception of the respective rôles of the architect and the engineer. In his view these are clearly differentiated, but precisely complementary.

Nowadays he has only one passion: his work, while his needs are largely confined to those of his profession. When he was at the height of his fame, he used to drive that fine "Voisin", with which some of his books have made us familiar. After the war he was seen about in a tiny apple-green "Fiat", but for some years the métro and taxis have sufficed for him. That this is a way of condemning the excesses of what he calls "automobilite" is certain, but one must also take into particular account the very "civilized" simplicity of doing without, which sometimes makes him inclined to forget how barbarous and unpleasant the "simplicity" of having to do without can be. He has been seen, in some town through which he was passing, trying to find two splendid masons whom he had met some years earlier on the chapel site at Ronchamp, with no other object than to pass the time of day with them. And there was that letter, which he illustrated, full of fun and charming perception, addressed by way of apology to a friend's cook whom Le Corbusier had not been able to congratulate when taking leave of his host. For things like these he can always find time, but for those which the artificialities of social life seem to expect of him he has little use. His passion for truth joins forces here with his liking for simple things, to alienate him completely from worldly occasions and formal conventions, being by nature hopelessly perplexed by what is "done" or "not done" in the higher social circles. To him ceremony is worthless when its value is purely decorative. In this there is something of that admirable, but somewhat over-rigid sense of integrity and of that wonderful, if reckless, refusal to compromise, which in the course of professional discussions leave him so often without room to manoeuvre, since they make any verbal equivocation impossible, even to save the situation.

Another faithful picture of "Corbu" and of the lines on which he thinks, of his characteristic susceptibilities and guiding principles, is provided by his frequent choice of certain words, especially in conversation. This is not affectation, but an expression of a remarkable feeling for order, at once logical and lyrical. Ordinary words, moreover, but with their form and stress modified in the end by Le Corbusier's constant and affectionate use, rather like muscles forced into exercise. Thus we find:

brave-type: does not mean "bon type"; but defines a man who, by creating beauty, is doing active good; reveals the moral pre-occupations of the speaker – Laurens and Léger were "brave types", Picasso is.

costaud: beautiful, but describing that noble, vigorous, strange, lofty, beauty which Le Corbusier admires.

digne: much used: suggests moral strength and rectitude in people – very close in meaning to "*costaud*" when applied to works of art.

dur: much used; almost always applied to the speaker's profession.

fatidique: defines as a rule the conclusions, attitudes or solutions imposed from time immemorial by certain facts of nature or history.

fidèle: describes those who are reliable and feel genuine affection. Friends and pupils may sometimes be "fidèles".

gentil: not to be confused with "modeste", but cannot be separated from it.

implacable: defines the character of anything which cannot be defied with impunity or from which one cannot escape. The laws of nature and history are always "implacables". "Impitoyable" is often used in the same sense.

joli: has no connection with prettiness; used when speaking of a beautiful thing, but with a certain quality of modesty and restraint.

poésie: much used; defines something which "has no set form, attitude or appearance", and applied to striking, unusual, "unpredictable" language.

politesse: a very rare and sympathetic quality.

sérieux: describes someone with the courage of his convictions.

solide: the opposite of spineless, fickle, unreliable. Close in meaning to "fidèle". Pupils are not so often "solides" as friends.

vérité: what nature always reveals when we know how to look at her.

Even when the portrait reveals flattering features which the model did not realize he possessed, we generally like to be seen as we see ourselves; and self-conceit has much less to do with this than the wish to be reassured – our peace of mind. We were quite happy with our own picture, or so we thought, and here comes somebody with another, which he claims to be faithful, but which bears little resemblance to the one we ourselves had built up so carefully in our imagination. This "portrait", friend "Corbu", may therefore displease you; I confess it will satisfy me if it succeeds in creating, if only in one heart, that deep, warm, feeling, compounded of admiration, respect, affection and gratitude, which all your friends cherish towards you.

Your life remains happy and full, although bitter, too – full, not of those frigid honours for which you were never cut out, but of that deep, sober, contentment, that wonderful richness, which a creative artist of your calibre always possesses naturally. Bitterness has come to you from others, from the invariable and endless difficulty of getting evidence admitted which is contrary to custom; but that is the inevitable lot of those who influence the course of history, who follow the slope, but in an upward direction; we may deplore it, but we cannot be surprised. Besides, universal approval for what you are doing and thinking would surely disturb you, since it is normally accorded, in your domain, to the false values of fashion and compromise.

It would be splendid, of course, if all those young men who claim to be your admirers and want you as their teacher, could compel the authorities to throw open the sites where your schemes are proceeding, so that they might have the honour of working with you and under your guidance. Unable so far to find an outlet for their eager and inspiring enthusiasm, some of them would do well to learn by heart and often repeat to themselves that letter, with its deep perception, humility and noble vision, which you wrote on 23rd September 1936 to one of your friends in South Africa. As the time comes for me to leave you, I have been reading it again. Let me therefore recall to them once more that "architecture is an attitude of mind and not a profession", that it is their duty "to give themselves so passionately to the study of the reason for things that architecture will rise as a spontaneous consequence" and that "by its inherent radiance, gaiety and grace, architecture will bring joy, and not merely efficiency, to the men of the new machine civilization". And you added: "Let this lamp be lit to-day *and folly be confounded*".

All this is fine, friend "Corbu", and your place is high and secure. Yet I am certain that you will never cease to feel that "poignancy of being alone and apart" which, for a young French author recently dead, seems to me to have been the glory and the mourning of a poet.

April-May 1960
Maurice Jardot

LE CORBUSIER

TEXT
AND
PLATES

Part 1

CHRONOLOGY

1900 - 1918
1919 - 1939
1940 - 1960

1

2

HOMELAND

1. La Chaux-de-Fonds, three thousand feet high in the Jura, was a place of refuge sustained by the victims of successive religious and political persecutions from the early middle ages until, and including, Russian pre-Revolutionary days. To this population was added, during the past hundred years or less, a host of artisans who came to work in the bars, and later (about 1900) in the large factories, which grew up as the clock-making industry developed, La Chaux-de-Fonds being one of its world centres from the start. **(1)**
To-day a town of 45,000 inhabitants, situated on the right bank of the Doubs, two miles from Franche-Comté in France. **(2)**

2. Its Charter was established at Rouen by an act of 2 December 1656 by Henry II (of Orléans Longueville), brother-in-law of the great Condé...
"Henry, by the grace of God, Sovereign Prince of Neuchâtel and of Valengin in Switzerland, Duke of Longueville and of Estouteville, Peer of France, Count of Dunois, St. Pol, Chaumont, Gournay Tancarville, Baron of Montreuil-Bellay, Vouvans and Mervans ... Lord of Coulommiers en Brie, etc. ... Governor Lieutenant General for the King and hereditary Constable of the Province of Normandy, to all whom this letter may concern, greeting..." Then follows the act of establishing the commune of La Chaux-de-Fonds: "...have granted and conceded to the inhabitants of the said Chaux-de-Fonds, and do grant and concede by these presents, the right of parish and commune..."

3. La Chaux means field, meadow.
La Chaux-de-Fonds means the last meadow on the slope of the Jura facing the West. A chain of mountains, about 5,000 feet high, defines the horizon. Beyond it lies Switzerland. **(3)**

4. There is La Chaux in Côte-d'Or, La Chaux on the Doubs, La Chaux near Alençon, La Chaux in Saône-et-Loire, La Chaux near Belfort, La Chaux en Poligny, La Chaux-des-Prés near Saint Claude, La Chaux du Dom Bief at Saint Claude, La Chaux-en-Bresse (Jura-Dôle), La Chaux en Lotière (Haute-Saône, Vesoul), La Chaux en Clairval (Doubs), La Chaux les Passavants (Doubs), La Chaux-les-Ports (Vesoul), La Chaux Neuve (Pontarlier), La Chaux-sur-Champagny (Poligny). (Taken from some 42,000 communes in the Atlas Quillet). These "Chaux" are situated on the west face of the Jura.

5. 1806. Field-Marshal Alexandre Berthier, Prince and Duke of Neuchâtel, on whom the title had been bestowed by Napoleon, opened a road between Franche-Comté (Le Doubs) and Neuchâtel over the mountains – a fine road "à la française".

6. In 1860 a railway was built in and out of the chain of mountains separating La Chaux-de-Fonds from Neuchâtel. A tunnel was pierced and the mountain rock caved in.

7. Rousseau and Lamartine passed through La Chaux-de-Fonds in the mountains of Neuchâtel. Rousseau wrote to d'Alembert: "I remember seeing in my young days ... a rather agreeable sight, and one that was possibly unique, a mountainside covered with homesteads, each of which was the centre of the land about it ... These fortunate peasants, all comfortably off, free from tithes and taxes ... cultivated with the utmost diligence their own holdings, of which they enjoyed the produce, devoting their leisure to making countless objects with their hands ... I continually admired in these people a remarkable mixture of refinement and simplicity, which one would have considered almost incompatible and which I have never noticed elsewhere ..."
Lamartine said that in these mountain farms he found Rabelais and Cervantes, Montaigne, Rousseau and Voltaire.

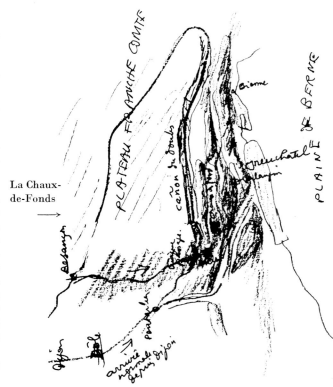

La Chaux-de-Fonds →

3 Sketch done from an aeroplane. 27 March, 1955.

8. Revealing details: the elder sister of L–C's father, on old lady given to religion of a sensible kind – it was the second half of the 19th century –, chided her nephews with words like these (L–C's parents did much the same): "Beau ténébreux, maritorne, rodomont, médor, matamore, artaban, malandrin, fier-à-bras, fanfaron, sacripant. Tire-larigot, godelureau, turlupin, fanfreluche, gringalet, cocquasse (casserolle)."

Some were from Cervantes, others from Rabelais, but nobody knew it, or cased about it, for this second half of the 19th century, before the coming of the machine age had already transformed men's minds. Such words were no more than traces, and had disappeared for good in the following generation. They were lost and forgotten, together with the deep reasons which had brought these peasant-craftsmen into contact with the masterpieces of earlier centuries.

9. And this maxim (cf. "La Royne de Quinte Essance", 5th book by Rabelais), "CE QUE TU FAIS, FAIS-LE", turned up again a few days ago at the foot of the card announcing the death of L–C's mother, Marie Charlotte Amélie Jeanneret-Perret, who died in her hundredth year on 15th February 1960: "Ce que tu fais, fais-le" ("Whatever you do, see that you do it"), the motto of the Gallet family of La Chaux-de-Fonds, who also came from the South of France.

4

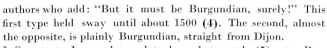

10. There is a very characteristic type of building in the Jura, especially on the highlands in the remote pasture country, a type sometimes combined with another characteristic of a totally different kind. The first is called "Burgundiàn" by certain local authors who add: "But it must be Burgundian, surely!" This first type held sway until about 1500 (4). The second, almost the opposite, is plainly Burgundian, straight from Dijon.

L-C went to Languedoc and took a photograph (5) near Bergerac, which is the exact image of the farms which he speaks of above, scattered across the Western slopes of the Jura, between the Jura and the valleys of the Doubs, the Saône and the Rhône.

The plan which follows is taken from the official work published in 1956 on the occasion of the Tercentenary of the creation of the

5

Commune of La Chaux-de-Fonds by Henry II d'Orléans. On the road across the high flat lands linking Franche-Comté to Neuchâtel, this map shows the "place known as: Les Jeannerets" (6). It refers to three houses from Languedoc which survived until the war of 1918, when they were burned down by accident. They stood behind a wall of rock called "Cul des Roches (Rocky Bottom)". In 1805 a tunnel was made through Rocky Bottom. But twenty years later the good people of the locality (Le Locle) asked the name Rocky Bottom to be changed to "Col des Roches (Rocky Pass)" for propriety's sake! The valley of la Chaux-de-Fonds marches on the Eastern side with that of Le Locle (of which "Les Jeannerets" was a part). The map shows a boundary mark at the "place known as: Les Jeannerets", where the lands of Morteau, Rochefort and Le Locle meet.

A relief map of France helps us to imagine what life was like in the middle ages in Provence and Languedoc in the twelfth and thirteenth centuries: the country was full of vagabonds and deserters, who pillaged and massacred the poor people ... the roads swarmed with destitute peasants, beggars and licentious soldiery; the glow of fires rose over the villages, and it was pitiable to see such beautiful country reduced to this miserable condition ("La Pierre Angulaire", by Zoé Oldenburg). (7)

11. The records of 1358 refer to the settlers who lived and farmed three thousand feet up in the Neuchâtel mountains. They had come from the plateaux nearby, a thousand feet below. The same records go on to record the presence at this place of "13 natives (others 'who were already there')". The origins of the Jeanneret family are known as far back as about 1600, when a fire at the church of Le Locle destroyed the local records. The Jeanneret may, therefore, have been among the "13 natives".

A significant fact: for centuries, and especially at the time of the establishment of the Commune of La Chaux-de-Fonds (in 1656), the name of Jeanneret never appears. Among the local worthies in 1657 we find: the Perret-Gentil, Robert-Tissot, Nicolet, Huguenin, Sandoz, Tissot-Vougueux, Du-Boz (called Cosandier), Humbert Droz, etc. ... From the beginning of the 18th century the Jeanneret clan had entered the general life of the community. We find a contract (of about 1800) between the factory of the Japy family of Beaucourt (in the Belfort country) and Jean-Jacques Jeanneret-Gris of Le Locle, which has to do with machine tools for the manufacture of clocks. The Jeanneret stock had spread so much that it was by now split into branches: Jeanneret-Grieurin, Jeanneret-Compas, Jeanneret-Gris. L-C is a Jeanneret-Gris. His father had an enamelling workshop. He was a pioneer of mountaineering, (almost all his life President or Honorary President). L-C's mother (a Perret) was a musician. His elder brother, Albert Jeanneret, is a violinist and composer.

6

7

"Jeannerets"

L-C from thirteen to seventeen years old, the tool of the watch-case engraver in his hand, or the goldsmith's hammer and chasing-chisel.

At the age of 17½, tackles the building of his first house (a villa, inside as well).

Client: l'Eplattenier. Nature study. The client was an emancipated pedagogue, and an emancipator. He was not a professional teacher.

At nineteen, L-C, pocketing his fees, sets out for Italy, and to see .... 1907 Budapest, Vienna; in Paris February 1908. Earned his bread with Auguste Perret (violently challenged by his colleagues at that time for acting as his own contractor, a crime of lese-architecture). 1910, retired to the mountains to study technical books on reinforced concrete. 1910, Munich, then Berlin. 1911, off Eastwards, knapsack on back: Prague, Danube, Serbia, Rumania, Bulgaria, Turkey (Constantinople), Asia Minor. Twenty-one days at Mount-Athos (Byzantine painting); Athens, Acropolis six weeks. The columns of the North façade and the architrave of the Parthenon were still lying on the ground. Touching them with his fingers, caressing them, he grasps the proportions of the design. Amazement: reality has nothing in common with books of instruction. Here everything was a shout of inspiration, a dance in the sunlight .... and a final and supreme warning: do not believe until you have seen and measured .... and touched with your fingers.

Such was L-C's school of architecture. It had provided his education, opening doors and windows before him – into the future.

A life spent in fifty-two years of struggles, failures and bitter opposition has not shaken the simple faith which he needed to lead the way into the unknown, nor has it barred the road which sometimes leads to a youth of a maturer kind .... a youth enduring and truly young.

.... 1914, the conception of the Dom-Ino houses. Already!

"New-section"
of La Chaux-de-Fonds
School of Art:
l'Eplattenier, director and
master of this very modern
class of instruction. Direct
inspiration of natural
things: 1900 to 1910.
Studies of rocks, plants,
roots. A watch chased in
silver, steel, copper, gold,
etc., by Charles-Edouard
Jeanneret at the age of
fifteen .... won the Diploma
of Honour at the
International Exhibition
of Decorative Art at Turin,
1902.
La Chaux-de-Fonds,
3,000 feet high, rugged
winters. Nature in the high
Jura. The fir became one
of the basic subjects for
study – that intractable
tree! In a purely accidental
and spontaneous way it
guided the young Charles-
Edouard Jeanneret (the
future Le Corbusier)
as far back as 1904, to
considerations of a
mathematical kind which
were to lead forty years
later to the Modulor.

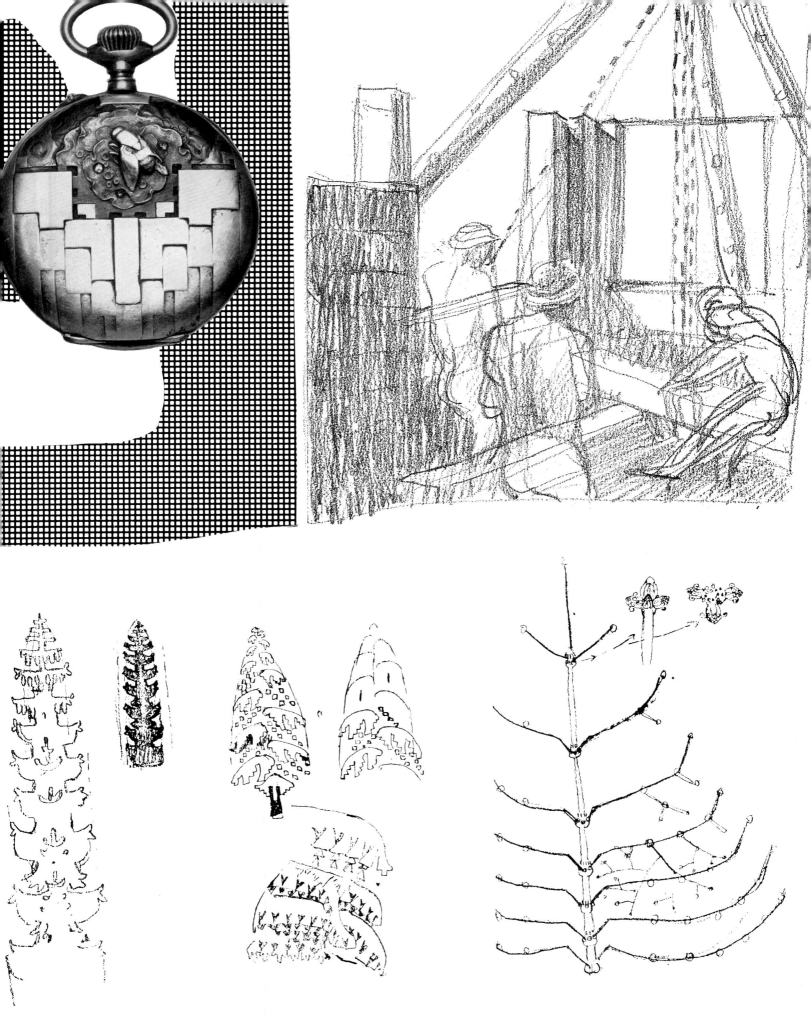

There was a magnificent book in l'Eplattenier's class library: "A Grammar of Ornament" by Owen Jones. Decoration is a debatable topic, but *"ornament"* pure and simple is a thing of significance; it is a synthesis, the result of a process of putting together. Making *ornaments* was a necessary discipline imposed by l'Eplattenier on L-C.

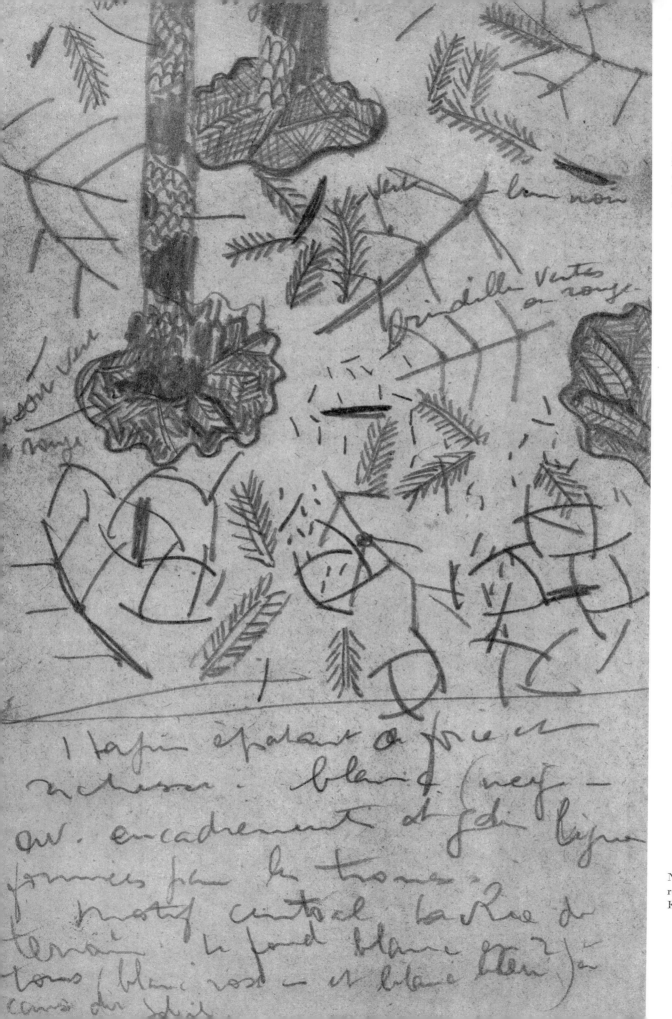

Snow lies under the pines in the forest. An extraordinary carpet of brushwood, tree trunks and moss.

→

Note: a characteristic representation of the Kaaba at Mecca.

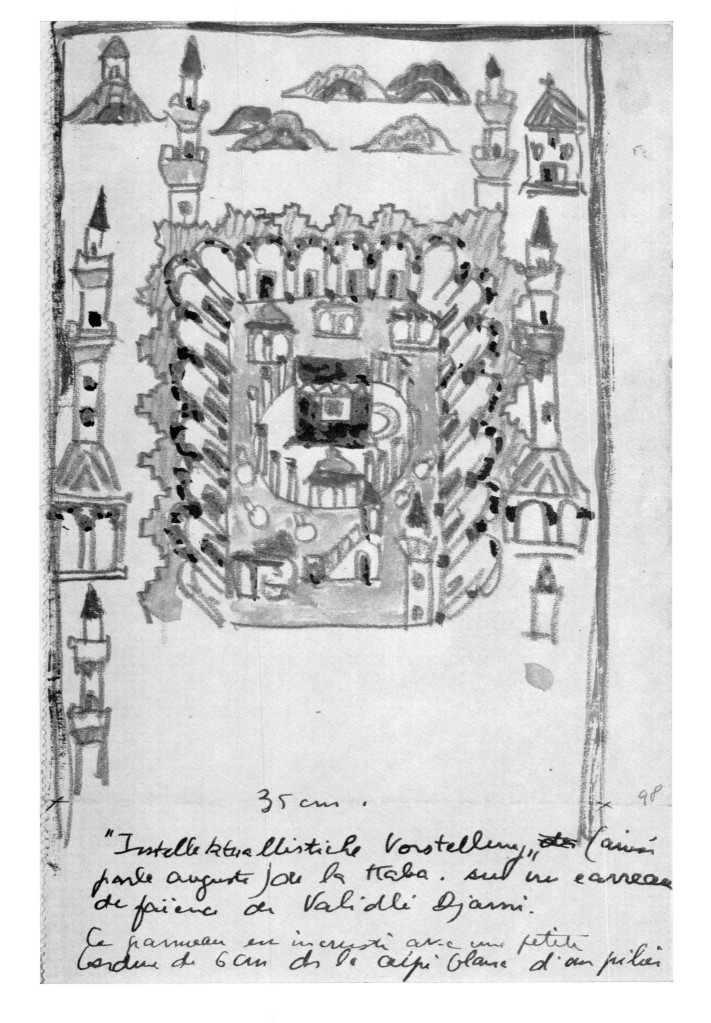

35 cm.   98

"Intellektuallistiche Vorstellung" ainsi
parle auguste par la Kaba. sur un carreau
de faïence du Validé Djami.

Ce panneau en incrusti avec une petité
bordure de 6 cm de la calpi blance d'un pilier

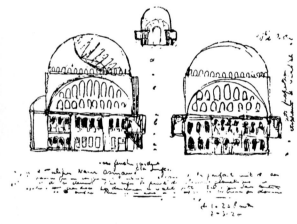

The walls of Byzantium,
the Mosque of Sultan
Ahmed, Saint Sofia,
the Grand Seraglio.
Come, you town builders,
note it down in your files:
"Silhouettes!!"

Turkish cupolas, daughters
of Byzantines:
Suléimanié-djarni.

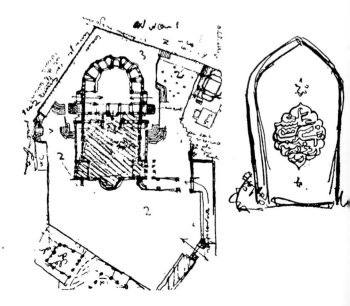

The Mosque of Doves ....
or of Tulips: courts,
porticos and even ....
rococo at Istambul!

Théophile Gautier's "hen coops": Turkish wooden houses
of the Bosphorus .... beautiful and imposing.

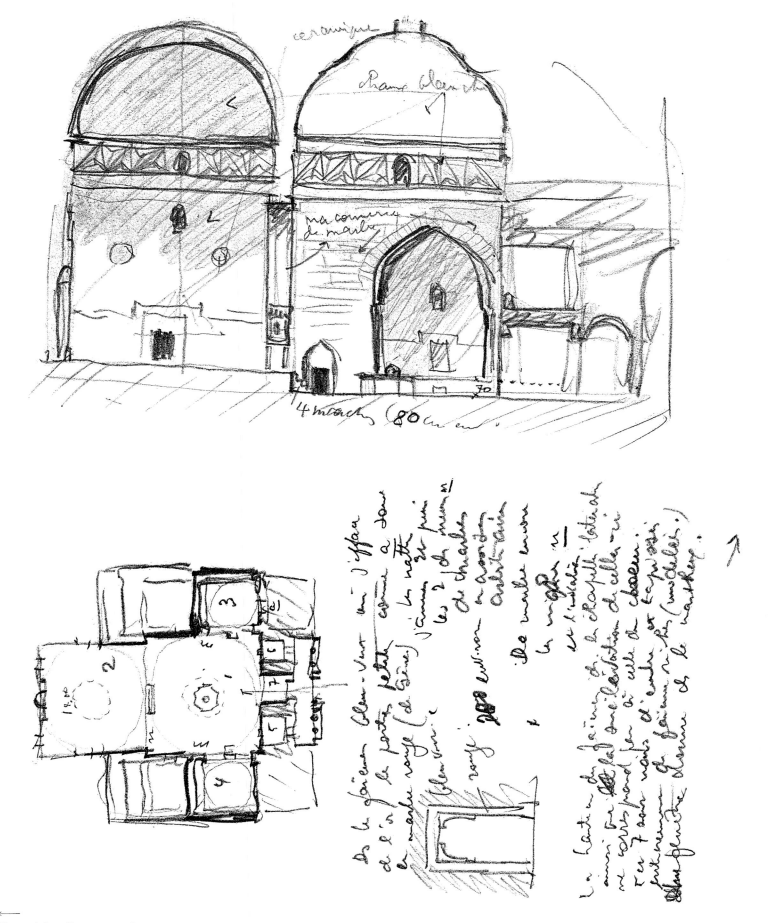

Mount Athos. Twenty-one days visiting fifteen monasteries founded about the year 800. Byzantine frescoes and miniatures. One noticed that in the course of centuries vandals had painted and repainted the frescoes, added beards, moustaches, gilding .... One day during the 1914 war some French officers from Gallipoli came and photographed the frescoes of Athos, using electrical projectors. They were able to illuminate the inaccessible corners which the vandals of other days could not reach; in this way some admirable frescoes were revealed, intact, in their original state.

The Parthenon appears (because it is off centre!) .
.... and the Propylaea disclose to one side the whole pan-
orama of the sea and the Peloponnese.

1911.
The Acropolis of Athens. What price Vignola and the Prix
de Rome? .... Where are those axes radiating from star-
shaped figures? Here are true dimensions .... very small....
proportion is what counts!

à l'opposé

When one travels and works with visual things – architecture, painting or sculpture – one uses one's eyes and *draws*, so as to fix deep down in one's experience what is seen. Once the impression has been recorded by the pencil, it stays for good, entered, registered, inscribed. The camera is a tool for idlers, who use a machine to do their *seeing* for them. To draw oneself, to trace the lines, handle the volumes, organize the surface .... all this means first to look, and then to observe and finally perhaps to discover .... and it is then that inspiration may come. Inventing, creating, one's whole being is drawn into action, and it is this action which counts. *Others* stood indifferent – but *you saw!* For instance, this landscape of Patras Missolonghi, Ithaca .... (here, on the left) on the North side of the gulf is a Greece bathed in limpid sunlight; a half turn in the opposite direction, and there is the dramatic vision of the Peloponnese. This scene and this contrast have stayed in *my* memory. If you draw the houses of Pompeii which you thought were *symmetrical*, because that was what your school taught you, your pencil will uncover some surprising asymmetries and some unexpected symmetries (look at the next two pages), too. When you draw the Tower of Pisa and show how sharply it slopes in relation to the cathedral and the baptistry, you will realise that this astounding phenomenon contains the very stuff of poetry. Explain it! *Try* to explain it to yourself! If you go to the Museum of the Castel Sant'Angelo in Rome, then draw the costumes of the Commedia Italiana: Arlecchino, Pulcinella, Pantalone; the brilliant contrivance, the style, of these theatrical properties will stay with you for ever. If you have seen Rome as a compound of horizontals and prisms, cylindrical and polygonal, you will have no mind to reproduce the obscene Punch and Judy show of pediments, columns, cupolas and axes radiating from star-shaped figures .... Even in drawing scenes of the Campo Santo at Pisa, you will have experienced the torments of hell; you will have witnessed crimes.

.... Apollo at Delphi.

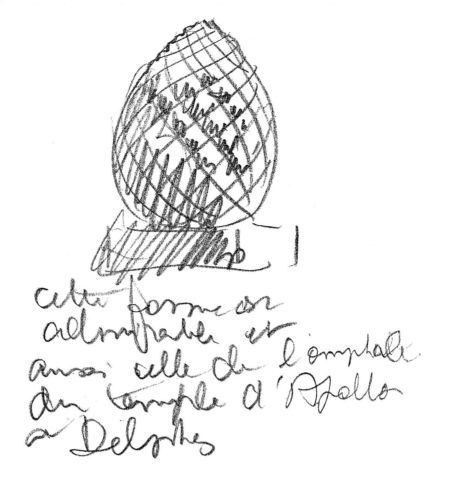

cette forme si
admirable est
aussi celle de l'omphale
du temple d'Apollon
à Delphes

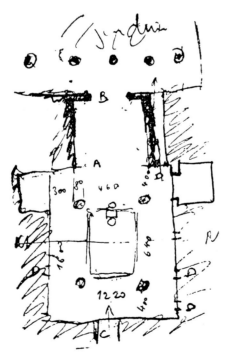

Pompeii. 1911.

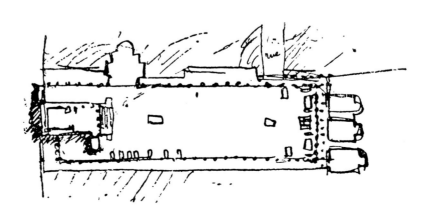

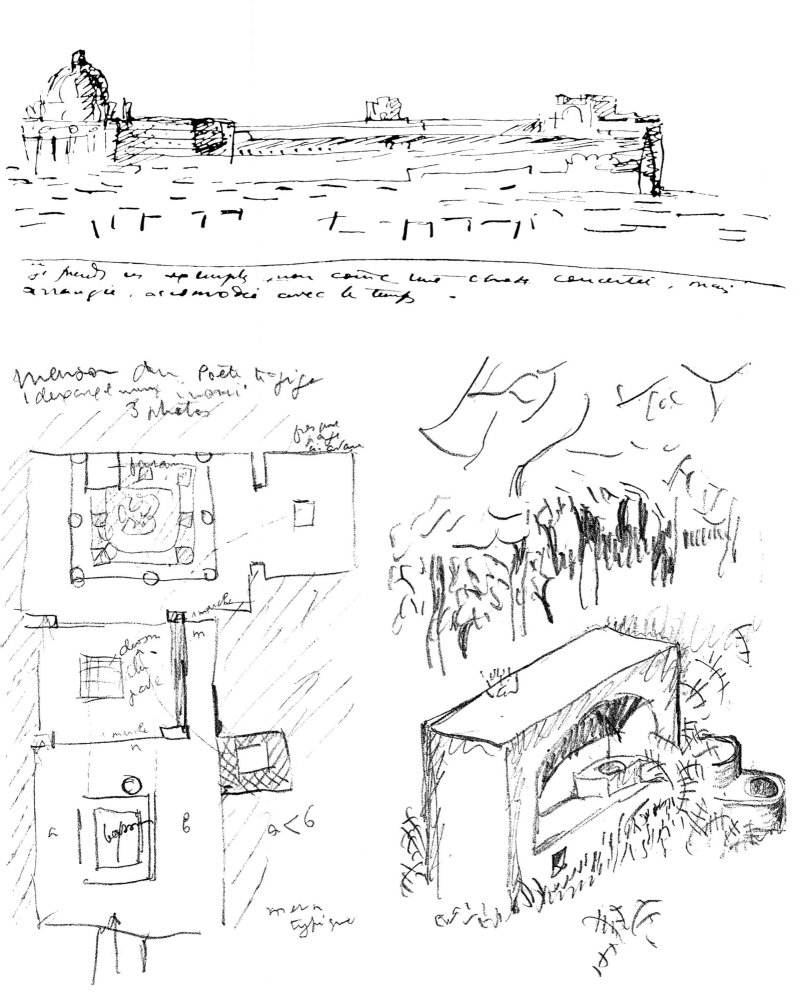

Rome.

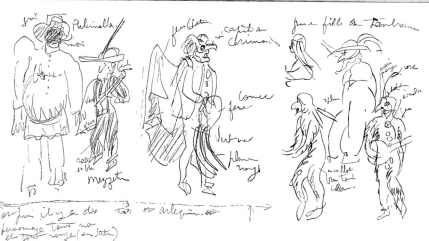

40

Pisa.

Landscapes of La Chaux-de-Fonds, touching perhaps, because uncertainty about life and the future was sheer anguish for a young man (before 1914).

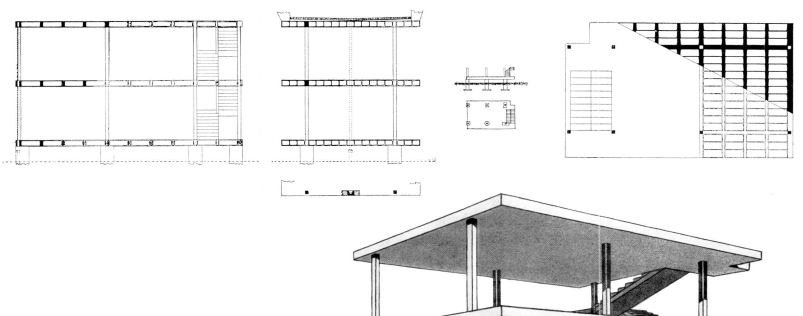

1914. Invention of the Dom-Ino houses, and a most unexpected invention at that time. A forecast of the potentialities of reinforced concrete, of mass-production, of human scale, of the modern factory. This type of building never found acceptance, either in reconstruction schemes after 1918 or since 1945. It was too new!

Arrival in Paris, the town which is never wrong, because it is full of things which have been loved, exquisite things, put there – never doubt it – with a sense of the sublime.

L-C has said: "Paris is the town which I have loved, and which I covered in every direction when I was twenty! Paris, whose fate to-day makes one shudder, victim of minds as trivial, as they are venal and conscienceless, sapping her very life blood."

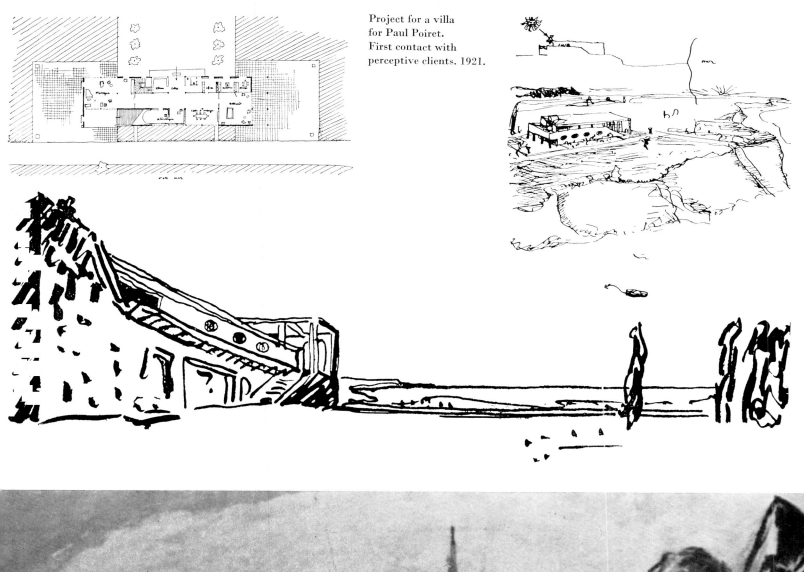

Project for a villa
for Paul Poiret.
First contact with
perceptive clients. 1921.

Chartres at night, when architectural sensibilities are most acute.

L'ESPRIT
NOUVEAU

1919-1939

L-C leaves his native town and sets up in Paris. Office opened in a beastly little street (Faubourg Poissonnière), seventh floor, over a yard, in a servant's room.

Auguste Perret gets Ozenfant and Jeanneret to meet. Ozenfant's prophecy: "Nothing will be built for forty years!" Thanks to him, Jeanneret started to paint at the age of thirty-one. His first picture dates from November 1918. It was an efflorescence of the landscapes of Greece: space and light (see page 220: "The Chimneypiece"). Space and light, the corner stones of L-C's character, the fountain-heads of all his endeavours. In 1919 "L'Esprit Nouveau" started publication, an international revue of contemporary activities. In introducing architectural problems, Jeanneret took the pseudonym Le Corbusier (L'Esprit Nouveau, 1920 No. 1). In 1921 Pierre Jeanneret joined L-C in the architectural section. In 1922 the grand study of a "Contemporary City of 3 million inhabitants" was exhibited at the Salon d'Automne. L-C's first buildings date from this period, after eight years occupied in designing and working out the technical means. In its first year, L'Esprit Nouveau published the series which in 1923 was to become the book "Vers une Architecture (Towards a New Architecture*)". It reached a world-wide public and was translated into English, German, Spanish, Russian and Japanese. The book contained: "Three Reminders to Architects": "Mass", "Surface", "Plan"; "Regulating Lines"; "Eyes which do not see": "Liners", "Airplanes", "Automobiles"; "Architecture": "The Lesson of Rome", "The Illusion of Plans", "Pure Creation of the Mind"; "Mass-production Houses"; "Architecture or Revolution".

On the very second page of this series there occurs this statement: "Architecture is the masterly, correct and magnificent play of masses brought together in light."

Received ceremoniously in 1929 by the State parliament of São Paulo in Brazil, L-C heard the speaker start by declaring: "When the first issue of L'Esprit Nouveau reached Brazil, we felt the impact of a great event ...." In 1925, the Pavilion of L'Esprit Nouveau at the International Exhibition of Decorative Art in Paris was erected in face of implacable hostility.

"The most effectively hidden pavilion in the exhibition", said the invitation card to the inauguration. The President of the International Jury (a great Frenchman) replied to his foreign colleagues who called for the Grand Prix d'Architecture for the Pavillon de l'E.N.: "It is not architecture!"

In 1927, after 65 meetings of the Jury at Geneva, the project by L-C and Pierre Jeanneret for the Palace of the League of Nations was the only one of 360 schemes (7 miles of plans) which received 4 votes out of 9. The others had only one. It was at this moment that M. Lemaresquier, the delegate from Paris, pointed out: "This scheme has not been drawn in Indian ink. It breaks the rules. I insist that it should be disqualified ....", and it was.

A world-wide protest by architects followed. CIAM [Congrès Internationaux (= International Congresses) of Modern Architecture] founded at the Château of Sarraz in 1928. During the past thirty years CIAM has altered the course of town planning (urbanisme) throughout the world.

In 1928 L-C and P. J. were commissioned to prepare a plan for the reconstruction of the Palace of Co-operatives

* Towards a New Architecture, Architectural Press, London; Frederick A. Praeger Inc., New York.

(Centrosoyus). As built, it differs from the original proposals. L-C devised "neutralizing walls" for this project, which provoked guffaws from specialists in Moscow (as in Paris). The physicist Gustave Lyon, however, declared: "It's a stroke of genius, which will transform architecture." He undertook detailed experiments at the St. Gobain laboratories, on which there is still a great file somewhere (at St. Gobain), which nobody has looked at since.

In 1928, plans for "Le Mundaneum" (promoter Paul Otlet) at Geneva, near the Palace of the League of Nations. Proposed again in 1933, for Antwerp. Forgotten. So much for internationalism. Madmen! And stateless persons!

In 1931, plans commissioned (in a limited competition – Auguste Perret, Peter Behrens, an Englishman (?), a Spaniard (?) and Le Corbusier and Pierre Jeanneret), by the government of the USSR for the Palace of the Soviets in Moscow. L-C and P. J were the winners. Then, suddenly, the decision was reversed. A senior official informed L-C: "Stalin has decreed that proletariat architecture is Greco-Latin in spirit." L-C's presence in Moscow to explain was considered undesirable. Since 1931 all contacts have been severed. "Blatant capitalist architecture!!! ...." Meanwhile L-C had some narrow escapes in Paris in the days of Hitler. His books were forbidden in Germany: "Bolshevist architecture! ...."

From 1930 L-C devoted twelve years to an uninterrupted study of Algiers and its future. In this city town-planning had not even been dreamed about in 1930. Seven great schemes (seven enormous studies) were prepared free of charge during those years at 35 Rue de Sèvres by L-C and P. J., with young assistants who had been coming since 1923 from every continent. A series of exhibitions of these schemes took place in Algiers. The public were plied with information. On one occasion a listener exclaimed: "If it was true, it would be built ...." All over the world the Algiers projects were published in the daily press and in reviews.

In 1929 L-C was invited to Buenos Aires by the magazine "Sùl" and by "Los Amigos del Arte" to present the problem of modern architecture and town planning. A series of ten extempore lectures was the result. Back in Paris, the book "Précisions sur un état présent de l'Architecture et de l'Urbanisme" was published. In his cabin L-C had written out, in retrospect, the ten lectures from the hundred large sheets of drawings done in charcoal and coloured chalks in front of his audience in Buenos Aires. The roll of these drawings is still in a cupboard of L-C's private studio. On the return journey firm friendships were made at Montevideo, São Paulo and Rio de Janeiro. Important friendships, too.

The ship and the aircraft have extended the horizon of the town .... The twenty plates of "La Ville-Radieuse" were composed. "Radiant city?" "Ville-Radieuse?" In the corner of each plate, two big letters, thus – V-R1, or V-R2, or V-R3 .... "What is this V-R?" somebody asked. The answer: "Ville-Radieuse". "Why 'radieuse'? It means nothing! Call it 'the locomotive'; it works like a machine!" No, "radiant", because those who want to say: "It's like living in a Prussian barracks", will have to prove it, and consequently look at the plans; and if they look at them, they will see that it is "radiant". And "radiant" is the sort of irresistible word which we ought to have to brighten our workaday vocabulary.

"*Les Unités d'Habitation de Grandeur Conforme*" are the keys to solving housing problems. From 1922 ("City of three million Inhabitants"); 1907, visit to the Carthusian monastery of Ema in Tuscany; 1910, second visit to the Carthusian monastery Ema; 1920 to 1960 (forty years of ceaseless research and comparative analysis of problems of architecture and urbanism, the "Immeubles-Villas", or "Unités d'Habitation", have graduated by their realism to a position of leadership. Plans for Algiers, Stockholm, Moscow, Buenos Aires, Montevideo, Rio de Janeiro, Paris (without a break between 1912–60), Zurich, Antwerp, Barcelona, New York, Bogotà, St. Dié, La Rochelle-Pallice, Marseilles up to (but excluding) Chandigarh.

1935; invitation from Rockefeller (Museum of Modern Art) for a programme of 23 public lectures on architecture and town-planning in New York, Boston, Philadelphia, Baltimore, Chicago and elsewhere .... 400 yards of architectural sketches, in charcoal and coloured chalk on six rolls of paper, were cut into 180 sheets approximately 6 ft. 6 in. by 4 ft. 6 in. in the course of this tour round America. Twelve years later in June 1947 (before the disreputable episode of the plans for the United Nations in New York), Mr. Nelson Rockefeller said to Le Corbusier at a private dinner at his home near Central Park: "You were the man who changed the face of architecture in the United States in 1935 ...."

In 1928 the two houses were built for the Weissenhof scheme at Stuttgart. Hitler denounced them as manifestations of bolshevism and wanted to demolish them. They escaped and, to L-C's delighted astonishment, were made historical monuments in 1958 by the municipality of the capital of Württemberg.

The same thing happened to the Villa Savoye at Poissy, built in 1929 and classified as a historial monument in 1959 (also without L-C's knowledge) by the French government (Ministry of Cultural Affairs).

1932–35 and 1937, years of misery, and of abject, blind folly by the profession and officials responsible for the International Exhibition of Art and Technics in Paris, 1937. When asked for ideas in 1932, Le Corbusier had proposed a comprehensive programme and a clearly defined objective: "The 1937 International Housing Exhibition". Four months before the exhibition, in December 1936, a site was at last allocated to him, but outside the real exhibition, an annexe at the Porte Maillot, in a country village (among cattle, horses and farm produce). L-C and P. J. erected their *Pavillon des Temps Nouveaux* of tentcloth, providing 16,000 sq. ft. of demonstration space for architecture, town-planning and housing expertise.

In 1928, plans for a *maximum-car*, providing occupants with the amount of room considered essential for both normal town use and long holiday trips (sitting or lying down), plus baggage, sliding roof, excellent visibility and safety. Packed with new features, including the results of aerodynamic experiments (published in March 1935 in a supplement to the Album de la Société des Ingénieurs de l'Automobile, devoted to the small car).

1936, return from the U.S.A. The book "Quand les Cathédrales étaient blanches (When the Cathedrals were white)" published, very friendly to the American people. Very friendly? Translated in New York ten years later in 1946–47, it was to be a best-seller, so they said! For years the American publishers' accounts have stated laconically: "sales: nil". The sub-title "A journey to the country of timid people" seemed rather charming in 1935 – but, to-day?

1935. A year spent in constructing the mock-up of a section of a "Ville-Radieuse". Modern living conditions.

1932. First photo-mural, 500 square feet, for the Swiss Students' Home (Pavillon Suisse), in the Cité Universitaire, Paris; denounced with unheard-of violence by one of the big newspapers of French Switzerland as corruption of the young.

1935. First mural painting (done for nothing by L-C in a house at Vézelay).

1938–1939. Eight mural paintings (free of charge) in the Badovici and Helen Grey house at Cap Martin.

May 1940, an external mural on an old building fitted up as "Youth Studios", a painting some 16×20 feet or so. The German occupation came and L-C left Paris. A "Beaux-Arts" architect took charge of the building and constructed a cloakroom right across the mural, sticking the roof half way up, and slap in the middle, with hangers for coats and hats in the painting itself.

1948, large mural, 500 square feet, for the Swiss Pavillon of the Cité Universitaire in Paris.

1951, double mural painting for Nivola on Long Island, U.S.A.

In 1936 L-C was invited to Rio de Janeiro at the request of Lucio Costa to review the plans for the Ministry of Education and discuss preliminaries for the University City of Brazil. L-C became a friend of Costa and of "Oscar" (1936), known nowadays as Oscar Niemeyer. First application of the "brise-soleil". In 1958 Lucio Costa was to tell L-C: "If your proposals for the bay of Rio had been followed, a splendid combination of architecture and town-planning would have resulted to-day." In the meantime Rio has developed on commonplace and undistinguished lines, to the city's detriment.

1937, Pavillon des Temps Nouveaux. Here was the solution to the housing problem (the "Unités d'Habitation"). Here was L'Ilot Insalubre No. 6 which would make way for the beginning of the great "East-West throughway" across Paris. Here was the Commercial Centre (La Cité d'Affaires). Here was a stadium for 100,000 spectators with its provision for a wide variety of activities: open-air cinema, open-air theatre, sports, dances, even speech-making: public celebrations .... At the inauguration of this huge pavilion, in the absence of the minister, in the absence of the commissioner general and in the absence of the architectural director, L-C turned to the guests and said: "Nobody has turned up. I therefore declare the pavilion open."

"The Paris Plan 1937" occupied part of the pavilion. It marked a stage. Another stage was to be reached about 1941 (see "La Maison des Hommes", published by Plon*; see "Les Plans L-C de Paris 1953–1922", Editions de Minuit).

The Pavillon des Temps Nouveaux included a comprehensive study of rural problems: the farm and the co-operative centre. Work done in collaboration with Norbert Bézard, an agricultural worker from Sarthe (and a man of solid worth). He died in 1957.

In June 1939, the Governor General of Algeria had announced in Algiers that he was willing to put into execution, starting in the autumn, the Commercial Sky-scraper of the Cap de la Marine (which L-C's last plan sited in 1941 on "Bastion XV"). After ten years of research this sky-scraper had developed a sound organic constitution and genuine architectural form. (See page 147.)

But, by the autumn of 1939, Adolf Hitler was threatening Paris.

The rest is silence.

---

* English edition: *The Home of Man*, Architectural Press, London; Frederick A. Praeger, New York.

"Still Life with Lantern", 1930. 39 × 32 in.

1918. Large sketch for Le Corbusier's first picture "La Che-
minée" ("The Chimney-piece"). L-C lost the use of his left
eye when doing this drawing at night: separation of the
retina. This first picture is a key to an understanding of his
approach to plastic art: mass in space. Space.

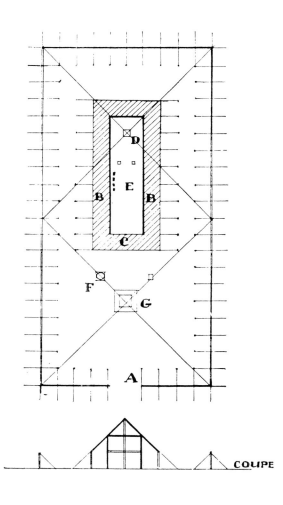

COUPE

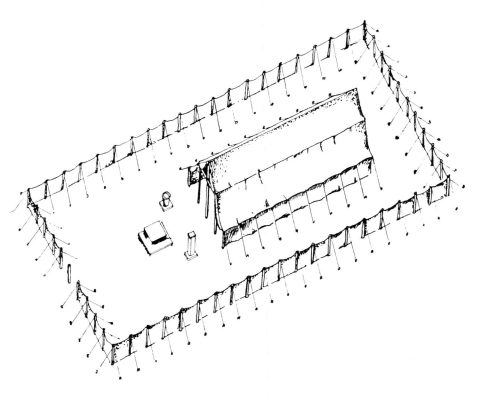

1923. BOOK

VERS UNE ARCHITECTURE
(Collection de l'Esprit Nouveau)
Edition Crès, Paris

"Fishing Port", 1919. Size about 36 × 29 in.

Note: *The dates of the pictures of this period, reproduced in "Number 6" of "L'Esprit Nouveau" in 1921, were muddled unbeknown to Maurice Raynal, who wrote the article, and to Le Corbusier.*

"Still Life with a pile of plates and a book", 1920. One version is in the Raoul La Roche collection in Paris; another is in the Museum of Modern Art, New York.

ARCHITECTURE

I

LA LEÇON DE ROME

ARCHITECTURE

II

L'ILLUSION DES PLANS

ARCHITECTURE

III

PURE CRÉATION DE L'ESPRIT

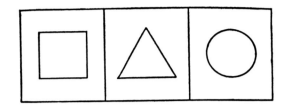

For five years "L'Esprit Nouveau" (an international review of contemporary activities) championed modern architecture and town-planning. "L'Esprit Nouveau" took its stand against decorative art and provided the material for books of the "Collection de l'Esprit Nouveau".

1921. CONFERENCES
"L'Esprit Nouveau"

Prag
Geneva
Lausanne

« Tout est sphères et cylindres. »

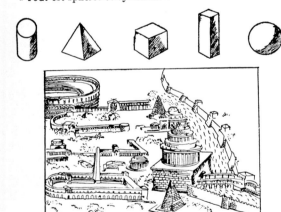

Il y a des formes simples déclancheuses de sensations constantes.

Des modifications interviennent, dérivées, et conduisent la sensation première (de l'ordre ma- 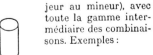 jeur au mineur), avec toute la gamme intermédiaire des combinaisons. Exemples :

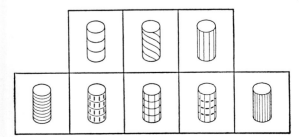

Voilà l'exemple d'un élément cylindre-primaire modifié systématiquement, déclanchant un jeu de sensations subjectives. En voici l'application et la demonstration.

Les mêmes propriétés géométriques gèrent les surfaces et déterminent le même jeu de sensations.

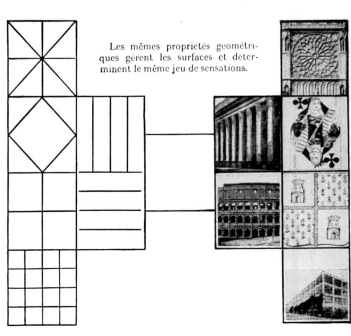

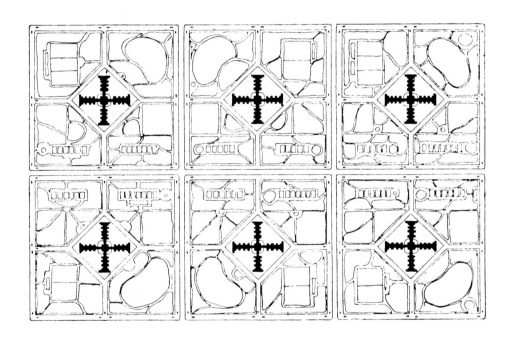

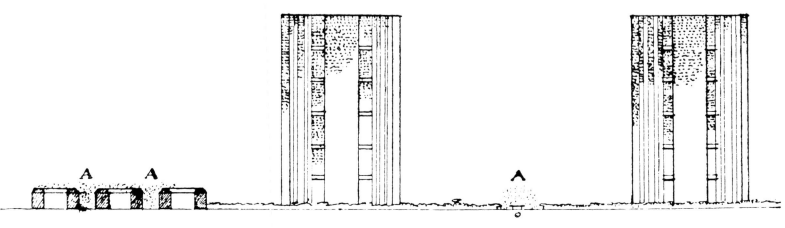

1922. This house at Vaucresson really marked the beginning of Le Corbusier's architectural research. Until then he had had no creative ambitions of any kind. He was thirty-one when he embarked upon a career which inspired a new approach to architecture.

"Still Life", 1922. Maurice Raynal Collection. Size approx. 22 × 18 in.

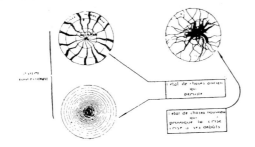

décongestionner le centre

UNE VILLE CONTEMPORAINE

J'ai dressé par le moyen de l'analyse technique et de la synthèse architecturale, le plan d'une ville contemporaine de trois millions d'habitants. Ce travail fut exposé en Novembre 1922 au Salon d'Automne à Paris. Une stupeur l'accueillit ; la surprise conduisit à la colère ou à l'enthousiasme. C'était cruement fait. Il manquait de commentaires et les plans ne se lisent pas par chacun. J'aurais dû être présent pour répondre aux questions essentielles qui prenaient leur raison dans le fond même de l'être. De telles questions offrent un intérêt capital, elles ne sauraient demeurer sans réponse. Écrivant cette étude destinée à la présentation de principes neufs d'urbanisme, je me suis mis résolument à répondre *tout d'abord* à ces questions essentielles. J'ai usé de deux ordres d'arguments : d'abord de ceux essentiellement humains, standarts de l'esprit, standarts du coeur, physiologie des sensations (de nos sensations, à nous, hommes) ; puis de ceux de l'histoire et de la statistique. Je touchais aux bases humaines, je possédais le milieu où se déroulent nos actes.

Je pense avoir ainsi conduit mon lecteur par des étapes où il s'est approvisionné de quelques certitudes. Je puis alors en déroulant les plans que je vais présenter, avoir la quiétude d'admettre que son étonnement ne sera plus de la stupéfaction, que ses craintes ne seront plus du désarroi

A town-planning section was organized at the Salon d'Automne of 1922. The head of the section came to see Le Corbusier and ask for his collaboration. "What is 'town-planning'?" asked Le Corbusier. "Well, it's a sort of street art — for shops, shop signs and so on; it includes such things as the glass knobs on the stair ramps of houses."
Le Corbusier: "All right. I will do you a monumental fountain, and behind it I will put a town of 3 million inhabitants." Le Corbusier forgot about the fountain and, with Pierre Jeanneret, made a detailed study for a city of 3 million people, from the standard dwellings and "Unités d'Hab-

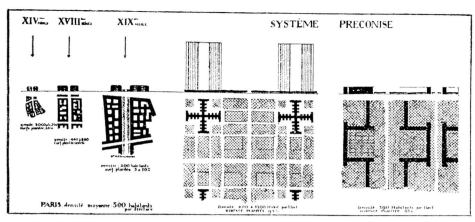

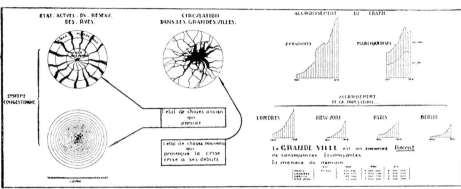

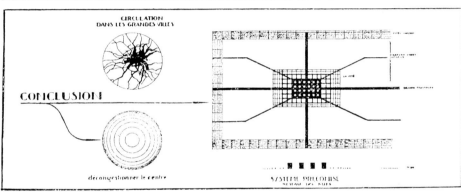

itation de Grandeur Conforme" to the avenues of the Commercial Quarter (Cité d'Affaires), etc. ...., contrasting his proposals with the confusion of New York. Léandre Vaillat, who edited a column in "Le Temps" on town-planning matters, wrote: "Le Corbusier is not French: the straight line is German: the curve is French ...." Bravo! But what about Versailles, Fontainebleau, the roads of Louis XIV and the roads of Napoleon .... On the same day, however, L-C met Blaise Cendrars for the first time. Cendrars was enthusiastic. They became friends.

1922. CONFERENCES
"L'Esprit Nouveau"

Basle
Zurich
Berne
Paris, Sorbonne

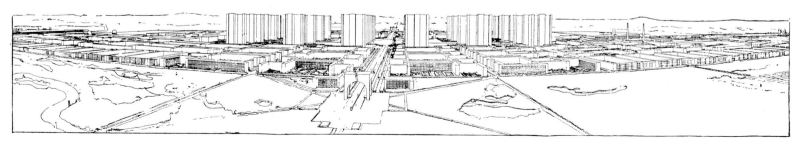

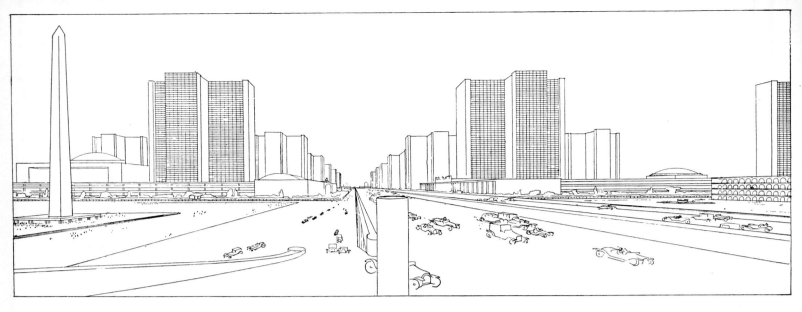

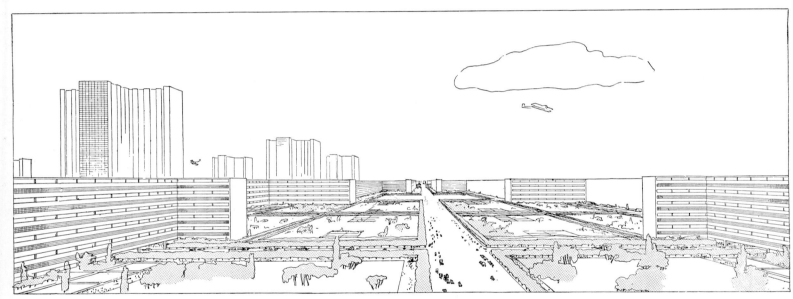

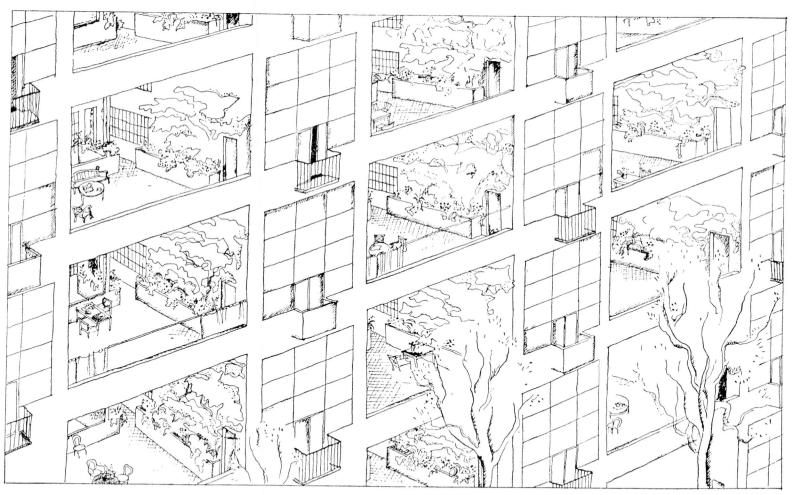

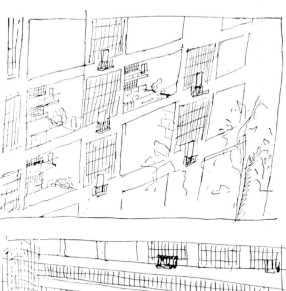

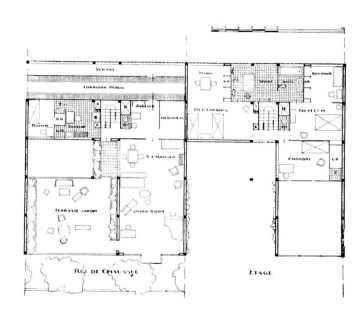

1922, at the Salon d'Automne, Paris: town-planning and architecture. Suddenly it had all come alive: the basic cell and the whole
conception. L-C had taken a mistress: HARMONY.

(See 1925, pages 72 and 73.)

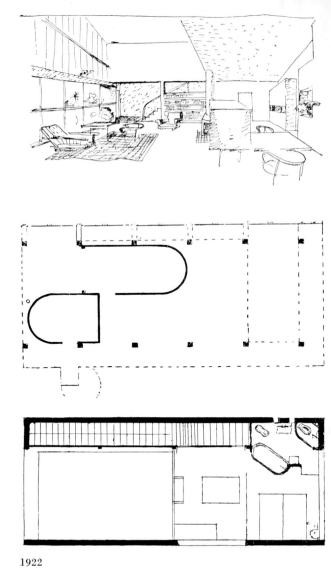

1922

1924. CONFERENCES
"L'Esprit Nouveau"

Brussels
Paris

1928. Two houses at Stuttgart for the Werkbund exhibition.

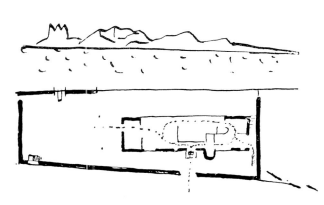

A little house on Lac Léman (Lake of Geneva). Officialdom, in the form of the Municipal Council of an adjoining commune, declared: "This house is a crime against nature; it must never happen again." 1923.

L-C
45

1923–24. "La Villa della Rocca" or, more precisely, the home of M. Raoul La Roche (built to form a pair with Albert Jeanneret's house). It was called "Villa della Rocca" to show that, given inspiration and an understanding of proportions, it was perfectly possible to create a building of manifest architectural quality, using the materials of workmen's dwellings. This villa housed the famous La Roche cubist collection.

Sitting room in Albert Jeanneret's house.

1925. BOOK

URBANISME
(Collection de l'Esprit Nouveau)
Editions Crès, Paris
English edition:
The City of Tomorrow,
The Architectural Press, London

These two adjoining houses gave rise to an entirely new "architectural polychromy": white, black, red, blue, pink, etc. ....

The Unité d'Habitation of the Boulevard Michelet, Marseilles, built thirty years later and an enormous building, relied upon a striking polychromy, both inside and out. Modern colour practice is a science in itself. The façades of the Unité at Marseilles entailed giving 4,000 instructions to the painters.

In India, in the capitol of Chandigarh, polychromy dominates the Law Courts and the Secretariat: black, yellow, green, red, blue, white.

The Le Corbusier "Electronic poem" of the Philips Pavilion at Brussels (1958), included a stupendous, coloured, electronic organ.

Architectural polychromy is a specific phenomenon, the natural spontaneous consequence (for the inventive mind) of the "plan libre" introduced by concrete and steel and by the organic conception of modern architecture.

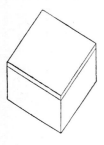

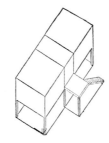

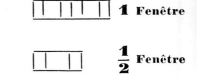
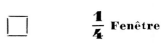

	1 Fenêtre
	$\frac{1}{2}$ Fenêtre
	$\frac{1}{4}$ Fenêtre

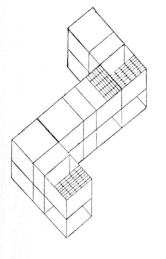
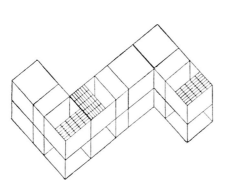
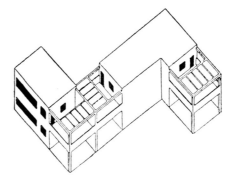
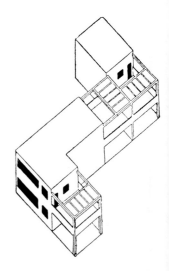

This scheme involved complex researches into standard-ization .... and an appeal to industry.

Garden-city of Pessac (Henri Frugès): 51 houses. Violent protests from the contractors and public opinion. Boy-cotted .... The town remained waterless, and conse-quently uninhabited, for several years.

APPEL
AUX INDUSTRIELS

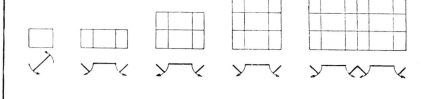

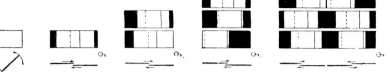

"Still Life with Violin",
1925. 39 × 32 in.

1925. International Exhibition of Decorative Arts in Paris: an exhibition of *mouldering plaster* come the Autumn! Pavillon de l'Esprit Nouveau by Le Corbusier and Pierre Jeanneret. Placard displayed in the pavilion, *"A call to Industrialists"* – *"The large-scale manufacturer must take charge of the processes of building"*. 1925–1960 = 35 years, about the time it takes to develop an idea and persuade public opinion to accept it. (See page 65.)

→

"It is not architecture" .... but in 1960, thirty-five years later, things like this are beginning to seem conventional.

1925—1927. BOOKS

L'ART DECORATIF D'AUJOURD'HUI
LA PEINTURE MODERNE (with Ozenfant)
ALMANACH DE L'ARCHITECTURE MODERNE
(Collection de l'Esprit Nouveau)
Editions Crès, Paris

1925. Proposed house for Mme. M. in Paris.

This house rose from garden to roof-garden opposite the park of the "Folie Saint-James", with its artificial ruin, and the pond which has reflected it since the days of Louis XVI...

"Monsieur, you are a dirty engineer, without soul or sensibility; you have no artistic conscience" recently cried certain poets and prophetesses.

The Stein house at Garches, 1927. The modern aesthetic at its sparkling best: the piers supporting this house, if placed together, would provide a reinforced concrete section 2 ft. 8 in. × 3 ft. 7 in. L-C wanted to use this as the motif (full size) for a mosaic in the hall. His client's reaction was: "Never! I don't want to know anything about it. I want to sleep at nights!" (He was a wonderful man, a splendid client, all the same: Gertrude Stein's brother. He had built (much of) the street car system of San Francisco — a tremendous job! And his wife had been the first to buy a picture by Matisse.)

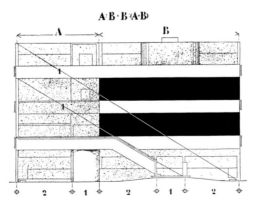

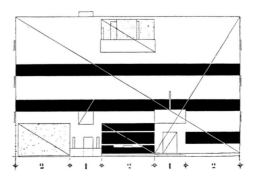

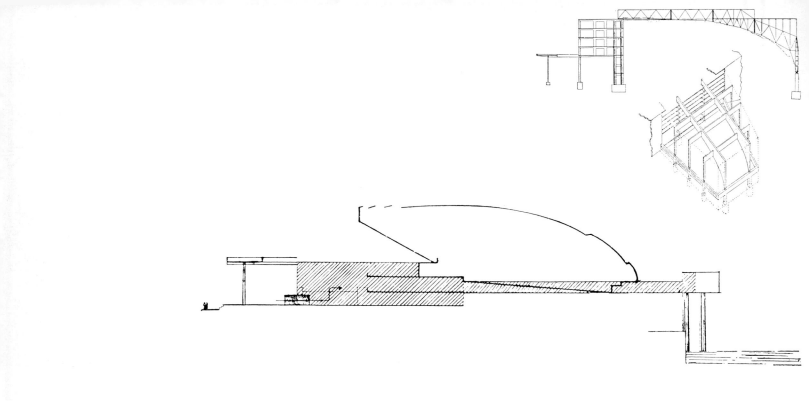

1927. CONFERENCES
"Une Maison – Un Palais"

Madrid
Barcelone
Francfort
Brussels

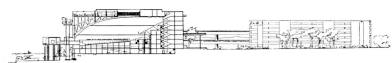

"These plans have not been drawn in Indian ink. I insist on their disqualification." (M. Lemaresquier, a member of the international Jury of the competition for the League of Nations Palace at Geneva, 1927.)

(360 schemes, 7 miles of plans, the project by L-C and P. J. being the only one nominated after 65 meetings of the Jury.)

1928. BOOK

UNE MAISON – UN PALAIS
(Collection de l'Esprit Nouveau)
Editions Crès, Paris

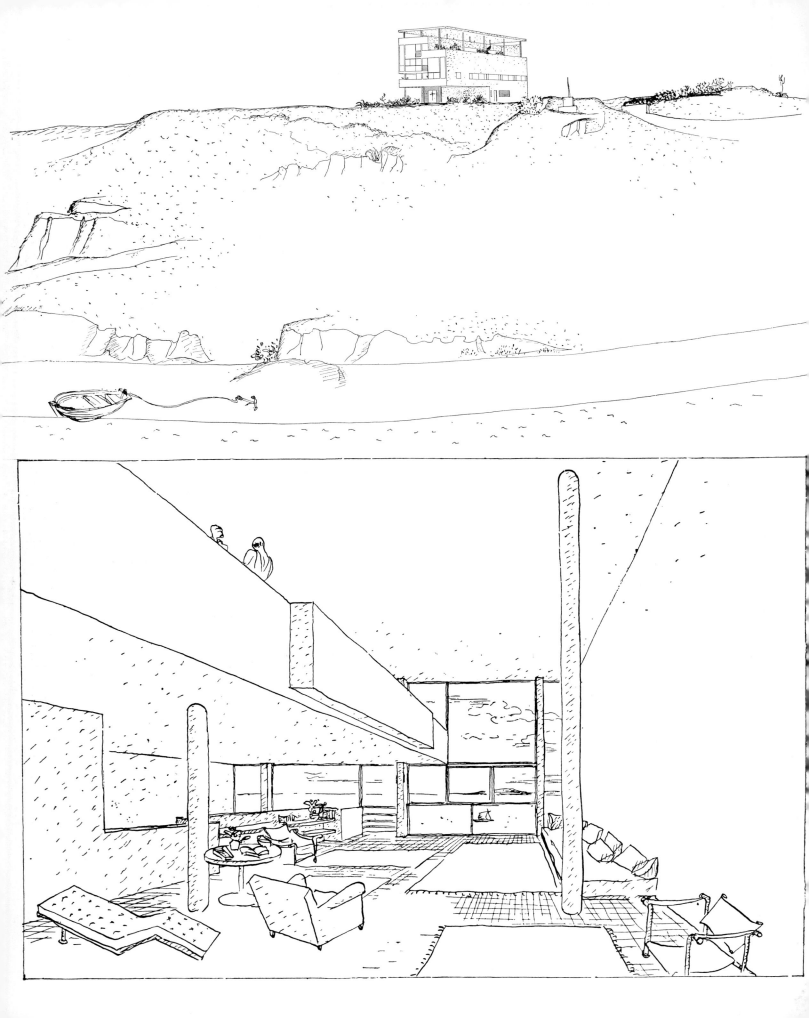

1928. House at Carthage.

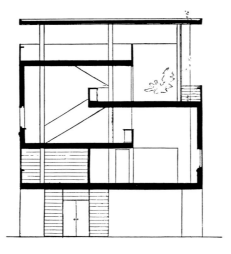

Expressive effect of the section.
Sunbreak (see High Court, Chandigarh, 1952).
Brise-soleil (see next page, number 3).

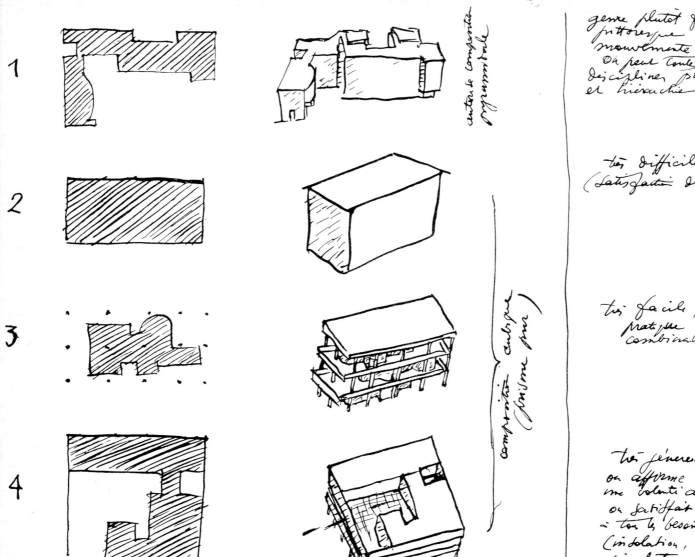

Some carefully weighed reflections on architecture:
1. La Roche.
2. Garches.
3. Tunis.
4. Savoye, Poissy.

Congrès Préparatoire
International
d'Architecture Moderne
au Château de la Sarraz
(Canton de Vaud, Suisse)

les 26, 27 et 28 Juin 1928

Ce premier congrès est convoqué dans le but d'établir un programme général d'action ayant pour objet d'arracher l'architecture à l'impasse académique et de la mettre dans son véritable milieu économique et social. Ce congrès doit, dans l'esprit des promoteurs, déterminer les limites des études et des discussions qui, à bref délai, doivent être entreprises par de nouveaux congrès d'architecture sur des programmes partiels. Le présent congrès a pour mission d'établir la série de ces programmes.

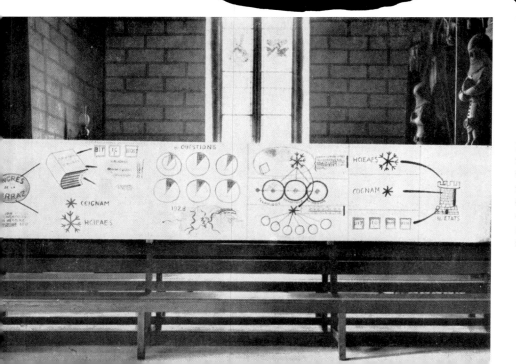

Foundation of CIAM (Congrès Internationaux d'Architecture Moderne). These congresses continued from 1928 to 1958, but have now been dissolved to leave the field to youth.

(The facsimile of the cover of the brochure which served as an invitation and a guide to the congress discussions, and also the poster which illustrated possible future activities of CIAM, are by L-C.)

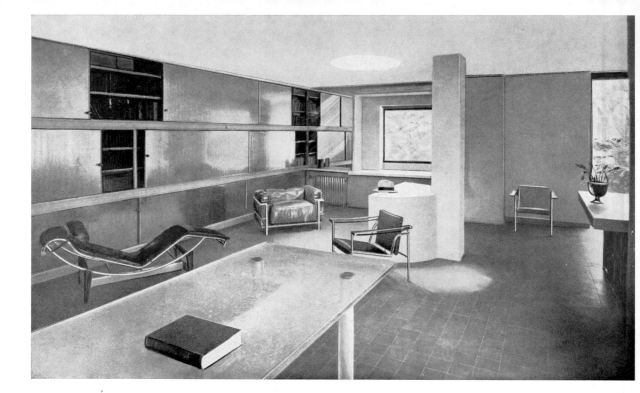

Modern furniture "1928".
In 1960 this furniture is in
production. 32 years ago
it was publicly displayed,
but...

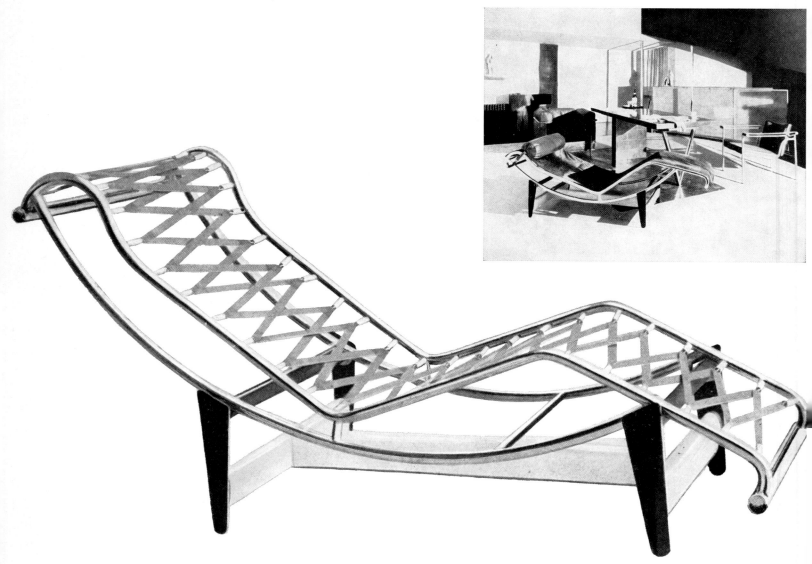

Painting "Lunch near the lighthouse", 1928. Size 39 × 32 in.

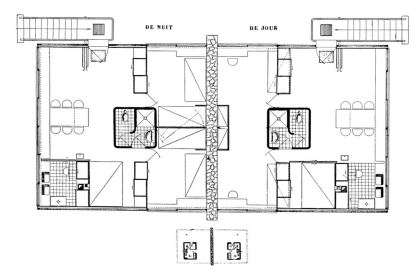

DE NUIT   DE JOUR

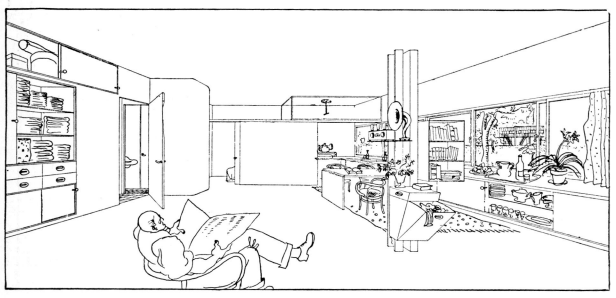

1929. So-called "Loucheur" house (400 sq. ft.). The delighted minister tapped Le Corbusier on the shoulder. "You will make thousands", he said. Le Corbusier: "No, Sir, we shall not make a single one!" "Why?" "Because your law has no real basis. There is no point of contact between the two sides involved: my plan (which is a way of life) and those for whom the law is made (the potential clients who have not been educated).

1929. The Mundaneum at Le Grand-Saconnex, near Geneva, above the Palace of the League of Nations: a first attempt at internationalism. Paul Otlet from Brussels, the promoter of the Mundaneum, had devoted his life and wealth to the project. He occupied premises in what remained of an exhibition building in Brussels (Palais du Cinquantenaire) .... One morning he was evicted with his typists, tables and papers. But he continued imperturbably with his correspondence until public opinion came to his support. Le Corbusier baptised him Saint Paul.

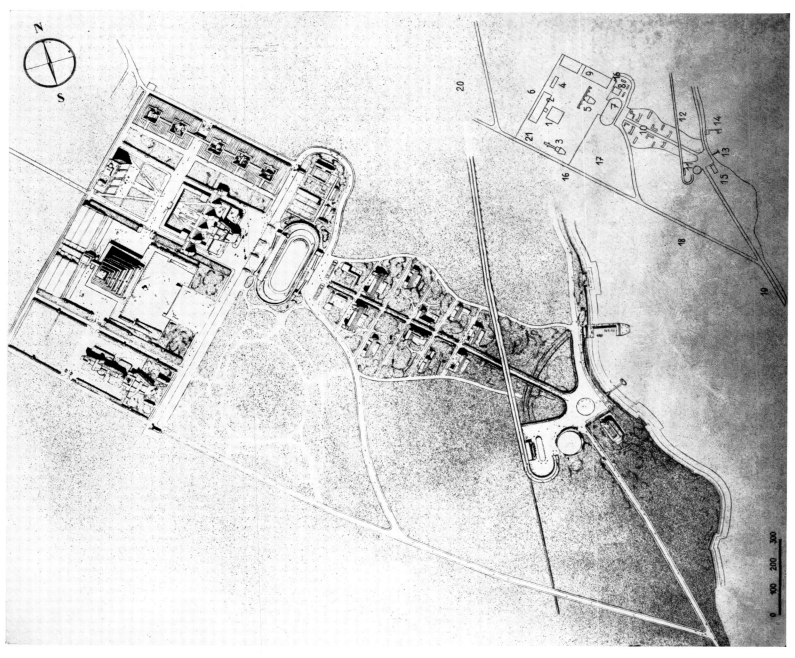

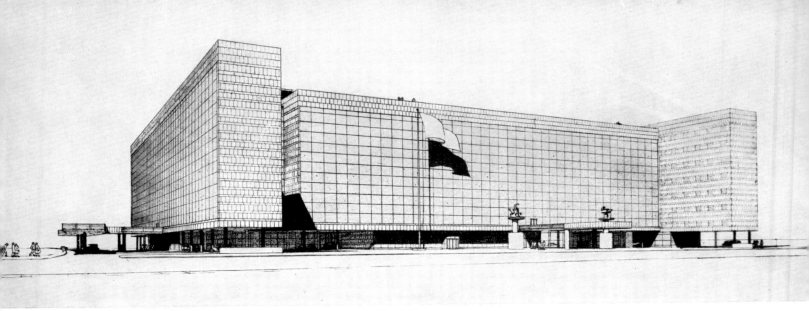

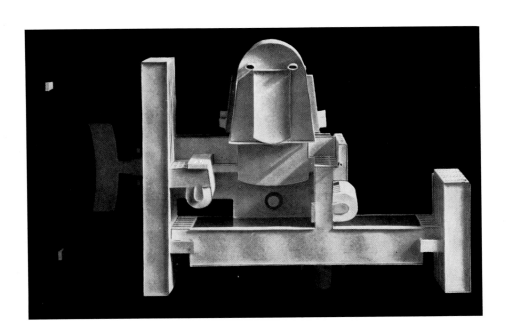

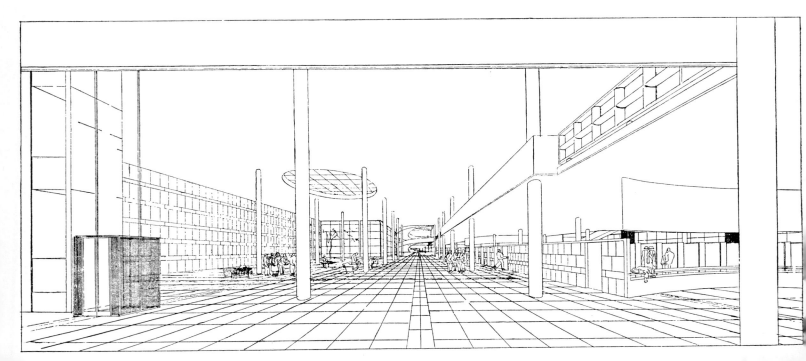

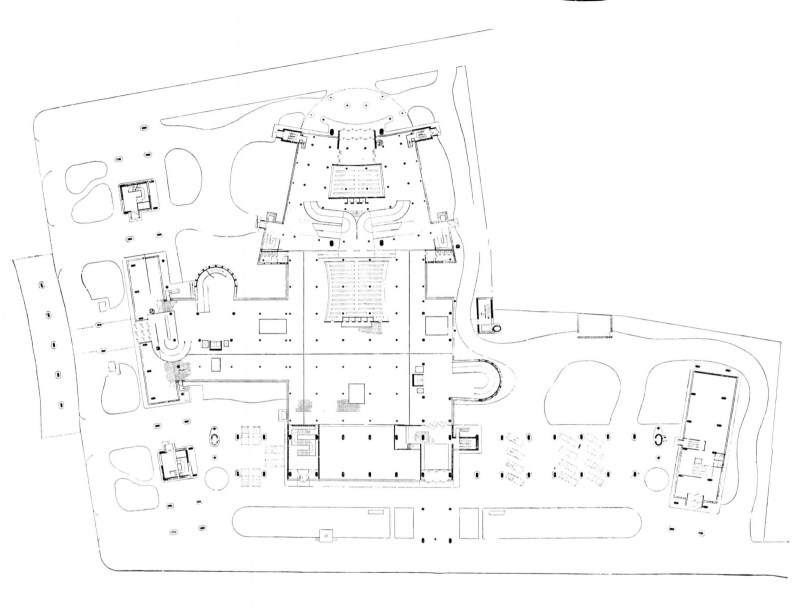

1928, Palace of the Cooperatives – Centrosoyus – in Moscow.
A beautiful plan!
.... and for every floor, too.

This plan, and the Swiss Pavilion which followed, and the Villa Savoye and the "Plan-Obus" for Algiers, which also came after, opened the way for the flexible, open, plan of to-day, the full-flowering of reinforced concrete. It possesses unique powers of architectural expression, an almost infinite richness. It has nothing in common with what has gone before, with the classical period (a room = four walls). Its ancestors, however, include Gothic. But Gothic was rigidly restricted by its plan and section and the technical imitations of stone construction; freedom came seven centuries later with the use of concrete.

(Note: "neutralizing walls" of glass or stone were designed for this building. This invention, which is a genuine, and indeed revolutionary, contribution to the art of building, has never been put into practice so far.)

"L'Immeuble Clarté", Geneva, 1928. A client risked it ....
the bankers smothered it .... but the building has survived.
As a matter of interest, Geneva has not been all that kind
to L-C's and P.J.'s schemes: Palace of the League of Nations, Mundaneum, "Clarté" building.

1929. CONFERENCES

Ten in Buenos Aires,
two in Montevideo,
two in Rio de Janeiro,
two in São Paulo
Paris
Moscow
Bordeaux

1930. BOOK

PRECISIONS
sur un état présente
de l'architecture et l'urbanisme
(Collection de l'Esprit Nouveau)
Editions Crès, Paris

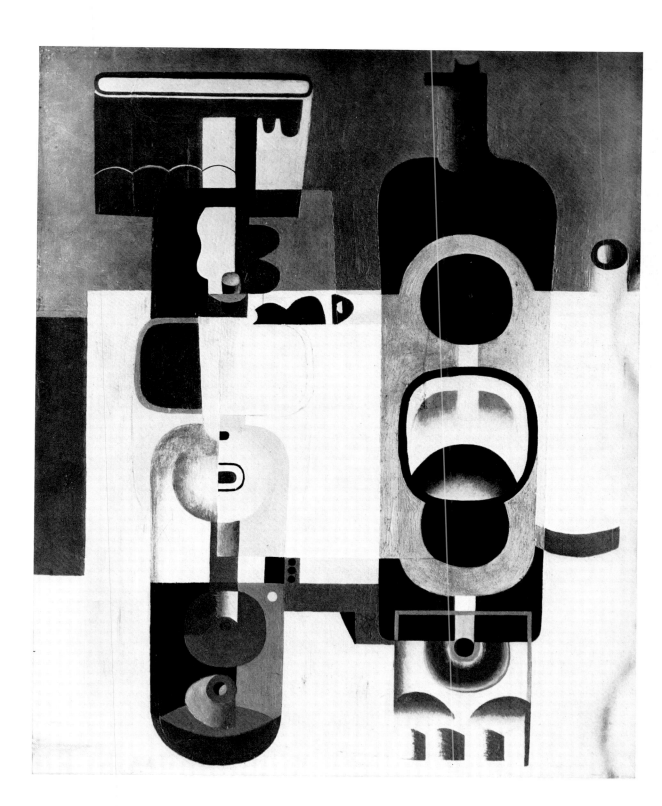

"Still Life: Two bottles",
1929. Size 39 × 32 in.
Exhibited in major
museums of Europe and
America since 1948.

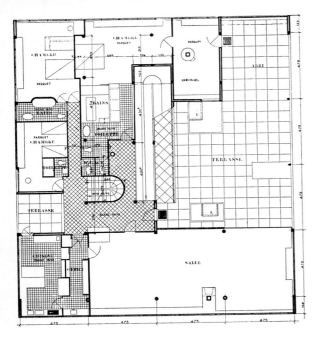

The Villa Savoye at Poissy, 1929, occupied by German and American troops (result: doors torn out and furniture removed!). Despite this, and whilst L-C was in India, M. Malraux, Minister of Cultural Affairs, had the house classed as "a historical monument", although French law only allows the dead to be honoured .... A young architect had heard by chance during a brief stay in Paris that the Villa had recently been acquired by the Commune of Poissy by compulsory purchase and was to be demolished to make room for a girls' school. He wrote, wisely, to CIAM, and within a few days 250 telegrams from the four quarters of the globe cascaded on to M. Malraux's desk.

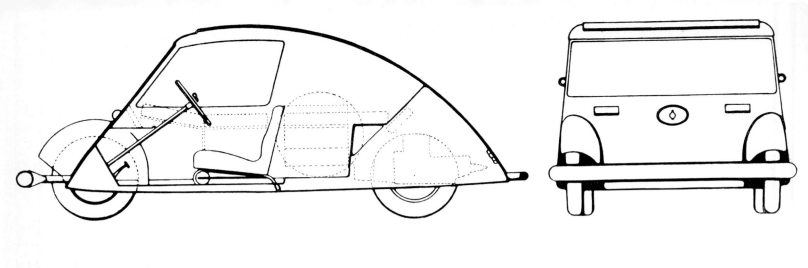

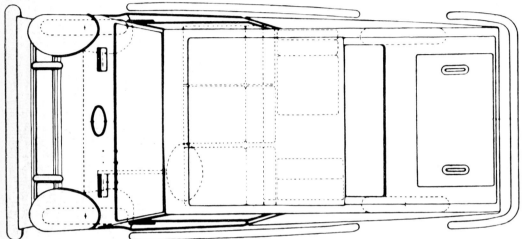

The authors point out that from 1928 onwards they had devised a type of car which they had no thought of promoting at that period, because it differed too widely from the prevailing notions of the time: engine at the back, aerodynamic design, lightweight construction, although with an extremely comfortable interior. The dominant idea was to provide the greatest possible comfort for the passengers; mechanical characteristics and construction being adapted to this fundamental consideration.

Passengers must have maximum visibility and be installed in an open, unencumbered space – a kind of belvedere (verandah or bow-window) – at the front of the car, therefore. They must not be inconvenienced by noise, smells (petrol and oil) and heat, or directly subjected to vibrations from the engine, which would consequently be placed at the back.

Plenty of space for luggage.

For long night journeys, the seats could be converted into couches.

Maximum space for passengers, by using the whole width of the car for the body (no running board or wings).

The external design, based on considerations of comfort, exemplified sound aerodynamic principles.

To reduce construction costs, the entire external face of the bodywork followed a simple curved line (pressed steel sheeting, lightly grooved).

The roof opened by a panel sliding to the rear.

To give passengers a feeling of safety, despite the rear-mounted engine, heavy bumpers (fenders) were provided in front, lighter ones at the sides and back. The interior fittings represented the ultimate in comfort.

Questions of weight-distribution, mechanical design, suspension, steering, road-holding, air-resistance, etc., had to take the above considerations into account.

(From L'Album de la Société des Ingénieurs de l'Automobile, devoted to a small car competition. These two pages formed a supplement to this publication, and the source of the text above is the Société des Ingénieurs de l'Automobile.)

→ "Hand and Flint", 1930. 38 × 51 in.

In 1928 L-C and P. J. designed a car which was called, not a "minimum-car", but a "maximum-car", providing the maximum efficiency for the user, while taking into account the possibilities of architectural expression within the technical limitations of the vehicle, its size, track and so on. These drawings of 1928 were published seven years later (1935) in a supplement to L'Album de la Société des Ingénieurs de l'Automobile, devoted to the small car.

The sequel: a discreet silence . . . . on the part of the beneficiaries. To-day (thirty years later) we see cars with similar lines.

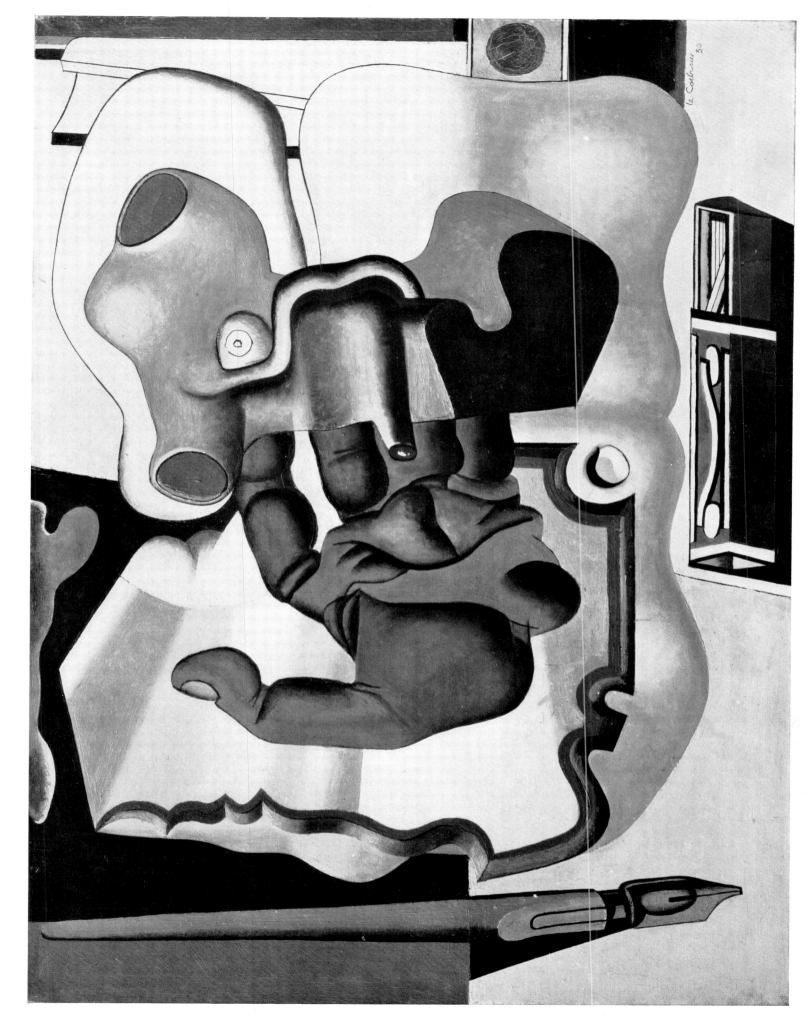

1930–1931. Swiss Pavilion in the Cité Universitaire of Paris.

The inauguration ceremony was like a funeral. Professor Fueter of Zurich University, a mathematician of international reputation, who had promoted the scheme for the pavilion, declared in his speech: "It is the finest modern building." Silence followed. The fanfare of trumpets was the only cheerful response. The President of the Republic, Albert Lebrun, on being shown round, said: "It is the first time during my term of office that I have opened a building which is finished apart from the plaster and pots of paint ....; there are even flowers on the tables and ash trays!"

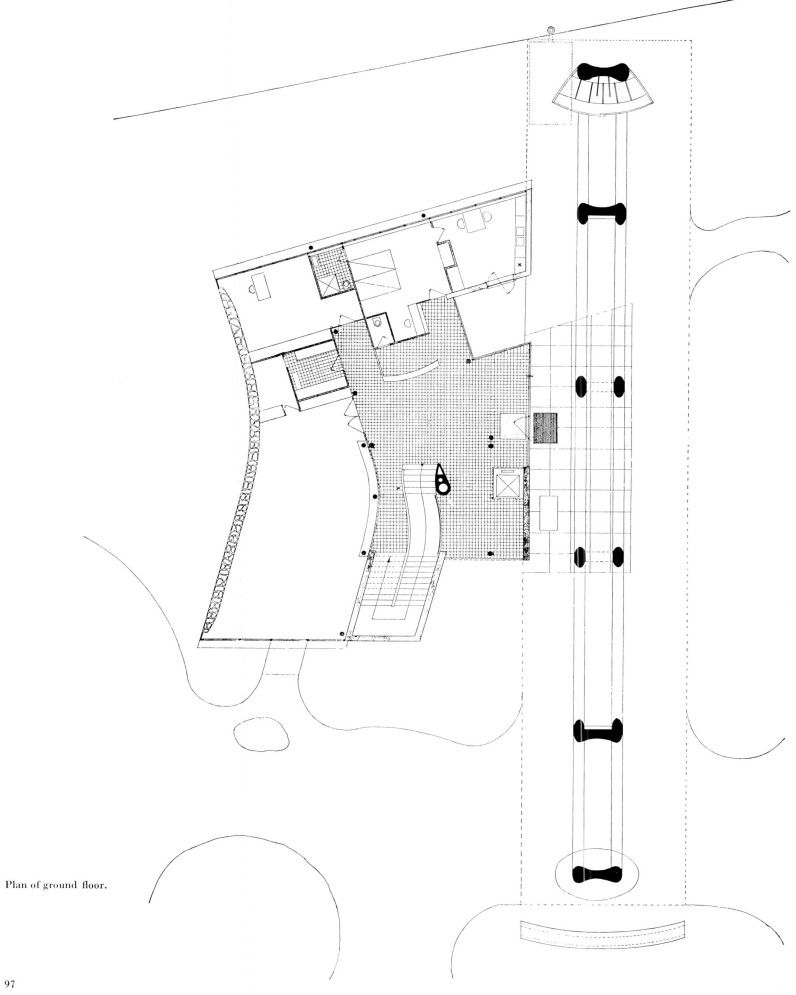

Plan of ground floor.

Same Swiss Pavilion: the library. Two days of deadly warfare raged over the curved wall of this room. Pictures of mountain scenery were produced and tried out, but it was established beyond doubt that the wall was curved and this was considered wrong. (L-C had made this wall curved to prevent pictures being hung on it.) Under dire threats, L-C thought up the idea of a "photo-mural". He had collected a mass of material with P. J., supplemented by views of microbiology and micro-mineralogy. These were blown up at frantic speed and stuck on the wall .... Scandal! The Gazette de Lausanne published two fulminating columns:

"That Swiss Pavilion again .... Were these pictures and the theories behind them referred first to any competent authority? And who, pray, are the men who dared to advocate their acceptance! .... We must surely be on our guard against what may with justice be called 'corruption of the young' ...." In my innocence, I had been guilty of praising the wonders of nature, the glories of Almighty God.

Fortunately (!) Hitler came and occupied the place in 1940, and had the photo-mural removed. But in 1948, Professor Fueter, autocratic and kindly, ordered from L-C a mural painting (of 500 sq. ft.) to replace it (see pages 230 and 231). L-C has since called it "the painting of silence", for silence enveloped it and envelops it still.

Fragment of the picture "Harmonie Périlleuse", 1931. Permanent collection of Le Corbusier's work at the Museum of Modern Art, Paris. 51 × 38 in.

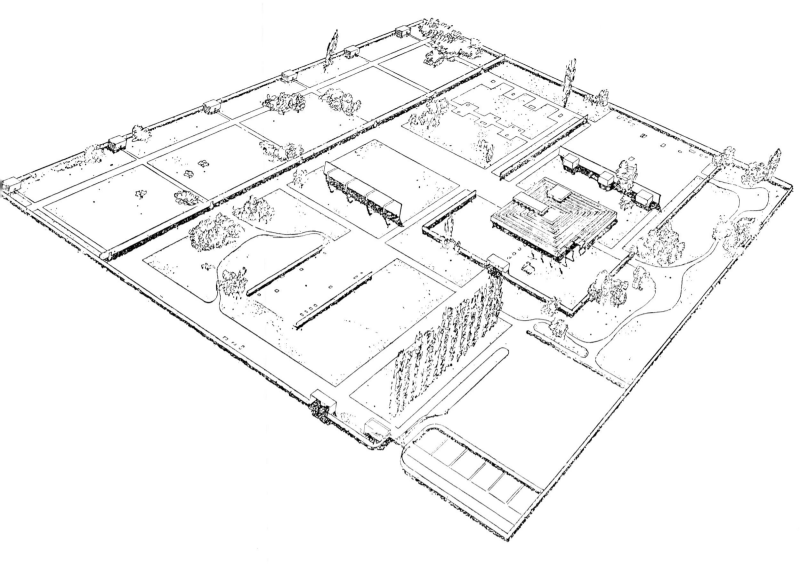

1931. Project for a Museum of Contemporary Art capable of unlimited expansion, to be built by a main road in a potato field: THE FRONTLESS MUSEUM: Starting in the middle, it would gradually extend in the form of "a square spiral". It was to be devoted exclusively to modern art.

This museum incorporated only one type of beam, only one type of support and only one type of window. One mason and a labourer, equipped with lifting tackle, could be permanently employed in building this museum in an uninterrupted and perennial operation.

The theory of the "Museum of Unlimited Expansion" was originated by Christian Zervos (a friend at one time) for "Cahiers d'Art", then taken up by the movement known as "Synthèse des Arts Majeurs" (an idea of L-C's for the encouragement of painters and sculptors). But it was pushed aside by aggressive interference from interested parties.

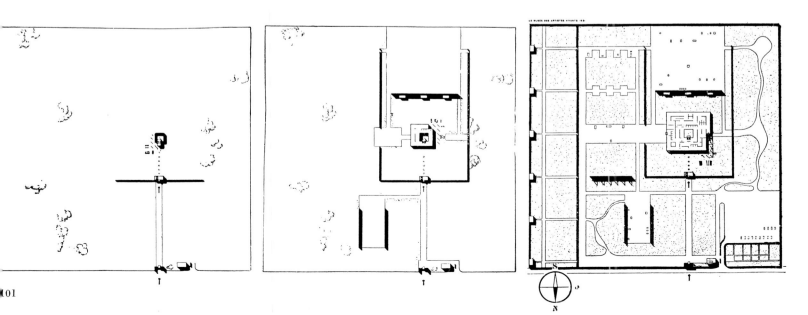

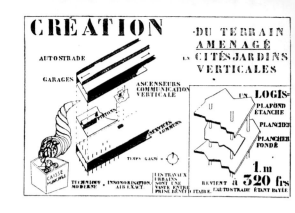

CRÉATION ·DU TERRAIN AMENAGÉ ᴇɴ CITÉS JARDINS VERTICALES

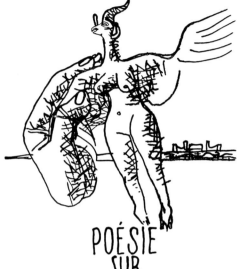

POÉSIE SUR ALGER

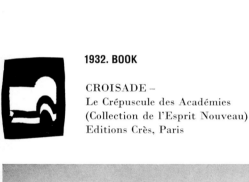

1932. BOOK

CROISADE –
Le Crépuscule des Académies
(Collection de l'Esprit Nouveau)
Editions Crès, Paris

1931. "Plan-Obus", Algiers. Twelve years of continuous work produced seven great plans for Algiers (1931–1942), which are well known in professional circles in every country. Reward:

At the time, Barberousse prison meant typhus within three days!
After 27 years (1957), the Algiers plan was truncated by .... friends.

"Plan-Obus", Algiers.

1931. CONFERENCES

Algiers
(from 1931–1939, constant public interventions)

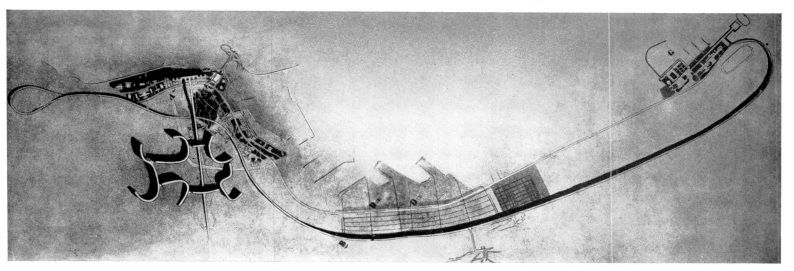

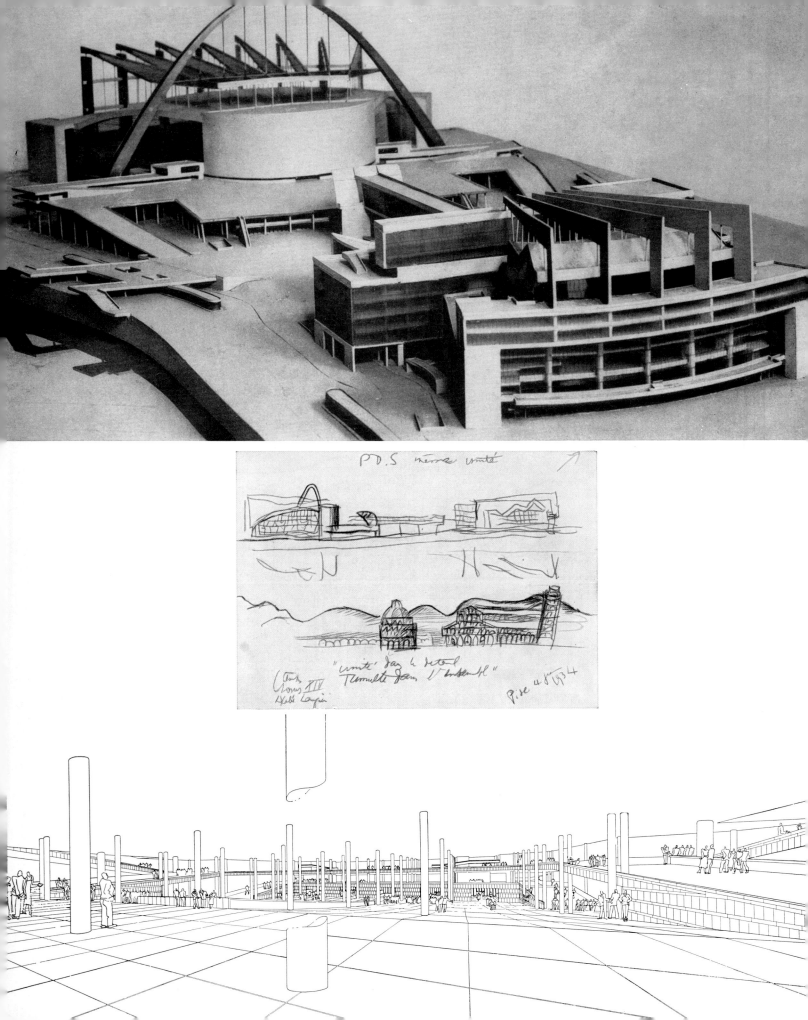

"unité dans le détail
Tumulte dans l'ensemble"

Pise 4 8bre 1934

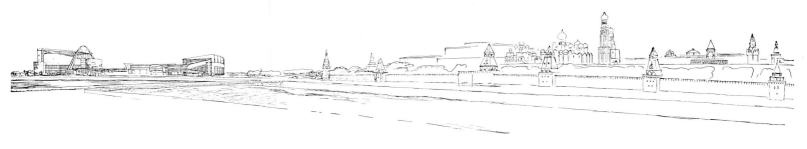

1931. Palace of the Soviets. Certainly the purest of L-C's designs. Had it been built, it would have been a wonderful thing. The hall for an audience of 14,000 was acoustically faultless (tested by light waves).

This palace represented a significant stage in the study of human scale. On 4 June 1934 L-C made the sketch opposite from a fleeting impression of the Campo Santo at Pisa, as he passed one afternoon in the train: the Cathedral, Leaning Tower, Baptistry and Campo Santo. The sketch above shows the outline of the Palace of the Soviets and a note which he made at the time: "P.D.S.: same unity."

The above photograph shows a splendid model, made in the studios at 35 Rue de Sèvres; and, a praiseworthy feature, all the important rooms are completely shown *in the inside of the model*. This went to the Museum of Modern Art, New York, in 1935, and toured the United States in travelling exhibitions, with the model of Nemours and the model of R.A. (Rentenanstalt, Zurich) .... It never came back!

The Salvation Army. The Rest Centre was long a place of pilgrimage for visitors to Paris. It was completely ruined after the evacuation of the German troops from Paris by the architectural incompetence of the staff of the Centre. The building can no longer be thought of as architecture.

1931. Building at 24 Rue Nungesser et Coli. Typical reinforced concrete structure with two glass sides, East and West. No protection against the sun. The seventh floor housed L-C's studio of "Patient Research". It was here (see the above photo) that the brise-soleil was invented .... and with good reason!

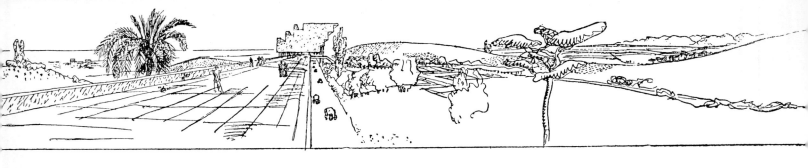

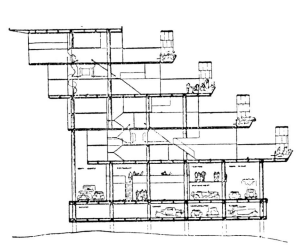

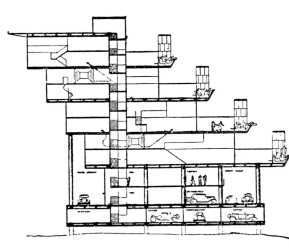

Planning the surroundings of Algiers. Improvement of agricultural land, vineyards, etc. Preservation of the landscape and of its cultivation, by the addition of architectural features which derive from the intrinsic difficulties of the site, such as, for example, the swimming pool placed under the pilotis, a device which was to be used later at Nantes-Rezé (see pages 171 and 273).

1933. CONFERENCES

Stockholm
Oslo
Gothenburg
Algiers
Antwerp

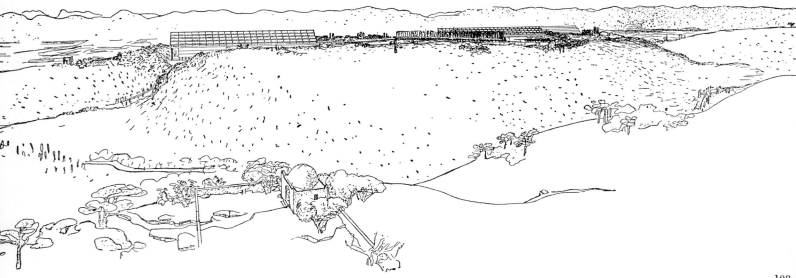

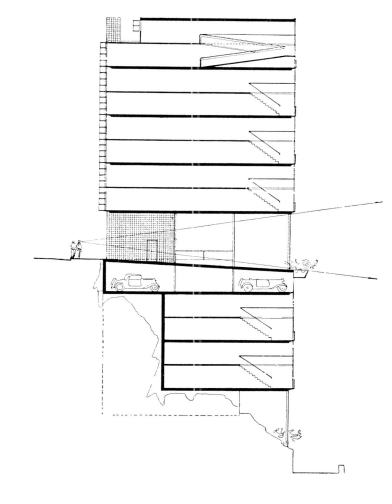

Algiers, the North façade *without* brise-soleil, but those South and West, *with*.

Note how the view of the sea appears between the pilotis, which are built on lower (and artificial) ground, and thus enable the capacity and volume of the building to be increased by at least a third.

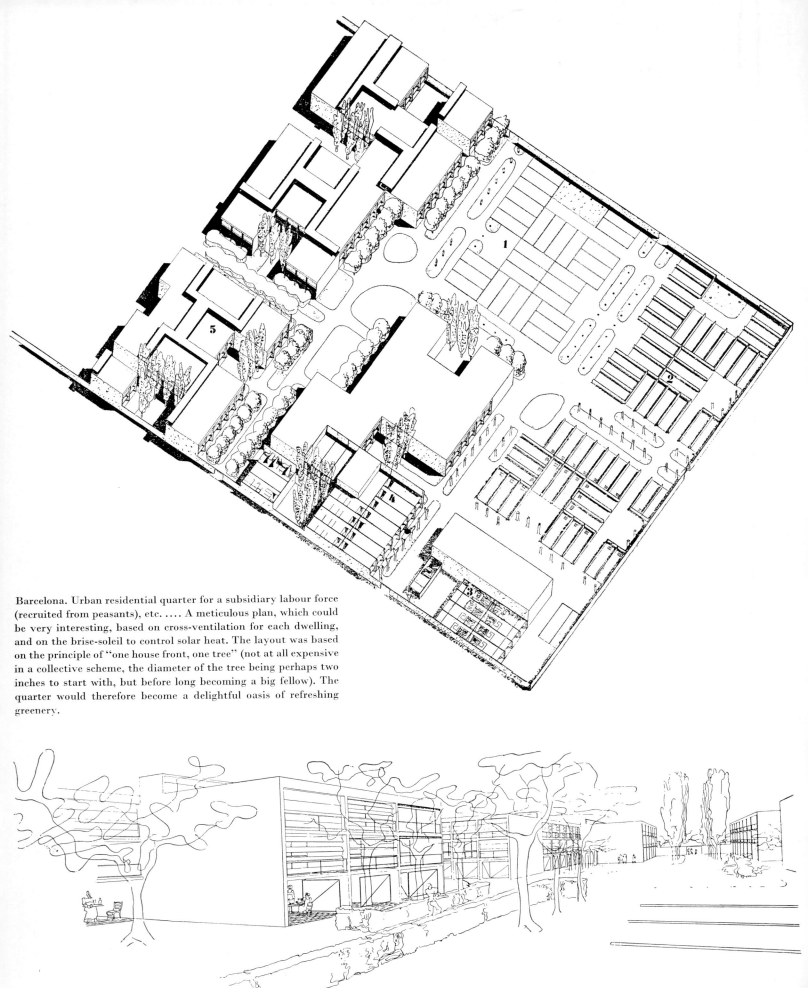

Barcelona. Urban residential quarter for a subsidiary labour force (recruited from peasants), etc. .... A meticulous plan, which could be very interesting, based on cross-ventilation for each dwelling, and on the brise-soleil to control solar heat. The layout was based on the principle of "one house front, one tree" (not at all expensive in a collective scheme, the diameter of the tree being perhaps two inches to start with, but before long becoming a big fellow). The quarter would therefore become a delightful oasis of refreshing greenery.

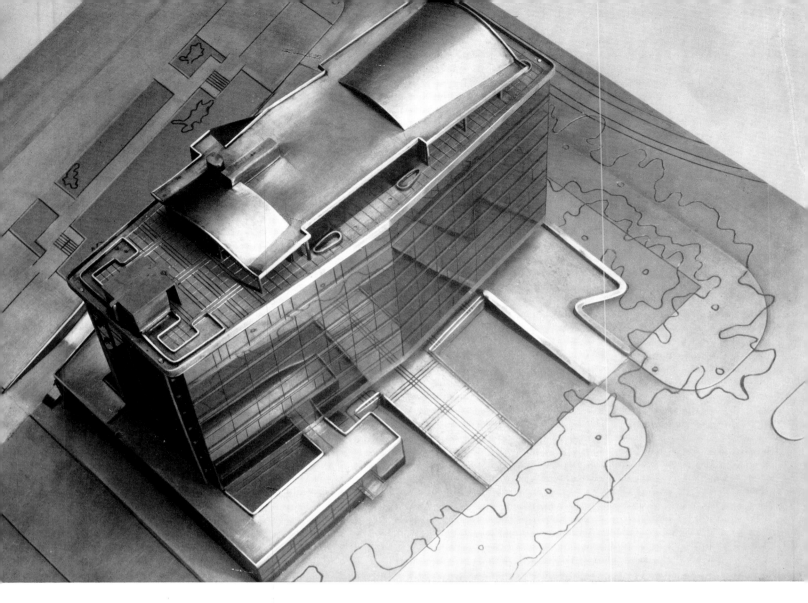

Rentenanstalt, Zurich. Insurance building on the lake. Still without brise-soleil.

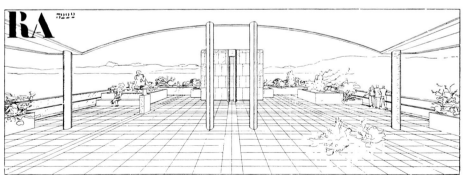

The Ministry of Education and Public Health at Rio de Janeiro, designed in collaboration with Lucio Costa and Oscar Niemeyer and erected during the war with Hitler, offers the first example of the use of brise-soleil in modern architecture. But a mistake was made. The horizontal panels of the brise-soleil are movable. The real principle is this. It is the sun which does the moving, never once occupying the same place in the sky for 365 days. A scheme can therefore be devised based on precise data: a) the course of the sun on every day of the year; b) problems of the latitude of the place under consideration; for instance, the sun must never touch a pane of glass during the summer period between the two equinoxes, but in winter the sun may be perfectly bearable. On the one hand, one absolute: among cosmic values; on the other, one relative: human predilections, freedom of choice. (See page 122.)

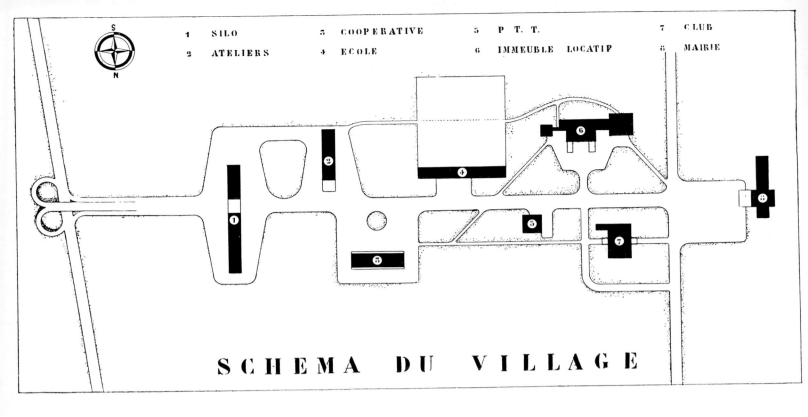

SCHEMA DU VILLAGE

For ten years L-C was very closely associated with people in the country, in particular with Norbert Bézard, an agricultural worker from Sarthe, a tower of strength in village life and perfect interpreter of rural needs in architecture and planning. The countryman is disheartened at being left outside the mechanical age and wants to establish contact with it. His problems found a response during the Occupation with the ASCORAL in the *"Trois Etablissements Humains"*; but it is only to-day, in 1960, that the fundamental position of the rural worker is seen in its true context, i.e., the countryman is as much a part of the technological age as the factory worker and the townsman. The creation of "La Ferme Radieuse (The Radiant Farm)" was the first result achieved. Industry provides the countryman with his tractor, his home, his byre and his barn. His wife, in her kitchen, is a woman of our modern world, also. The series of studies was devoted to the "Co-operative Centre" and introduced a new geography to the farm.

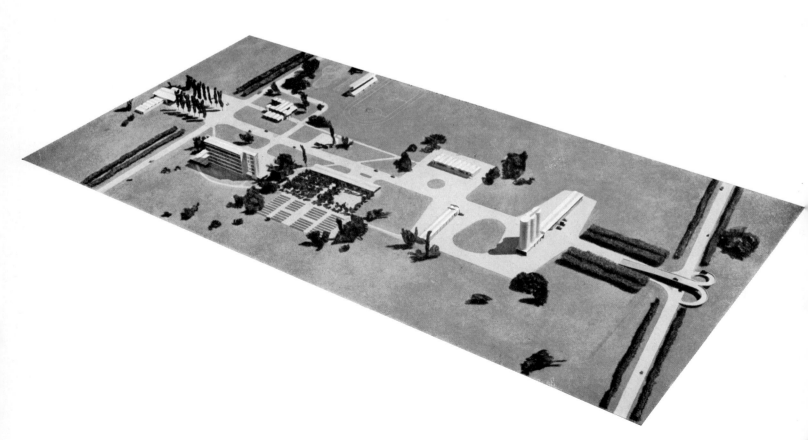

112

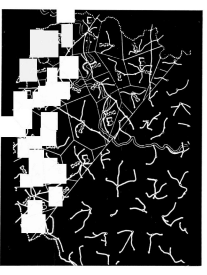

Department of Sarthe: example of the grouping of villages round a Co-operative Centre.

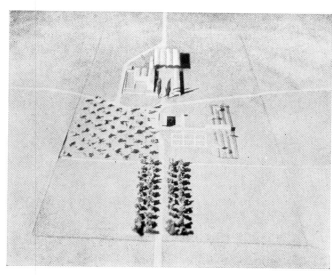

Agrarian Reform = la Ferme Radieuse (Radiant Farm), the Co-operative Centre. Studies of Paris, Stockholm, New York, Moscow, Antwerp, etc. ... had laid bare the mechanism of towns and made it possible to see inside. Studies of the modern farm, with the countryman's Home and Co-operative Centre, with tractors and the favourable consequences which they brought, had led twenty years later to the formulation of the law of the "Trois Etablissements Humains" (with its great promise for modern times, which makes possible a truly effective use of land, and which will weld into a harmonious whole agricultural and industrial production and the interchange of goods and ideas).

For fifteen years, amid indifference and sneers, studies proceeded with Norbert Bézard, an agricultural worker from Sarthe and a great driving force. The use of the tractor, hard-surfaced roads, a logical systemization of the farm site, Co-operative Centres ... were among matters advocated.

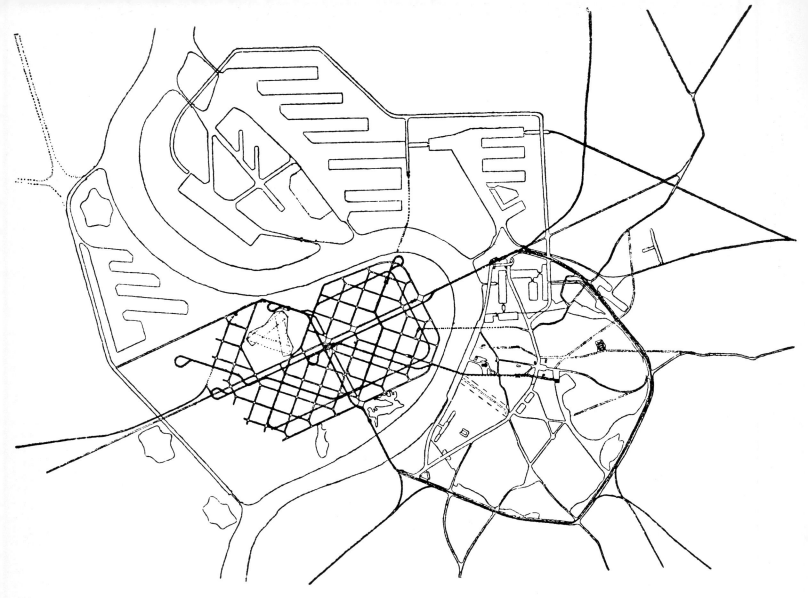

1934. CONFERENCES

Rome
Milan
Algiers
Barcelone
Athens

1933. Antwerp Plan. 150 feet of studies, worked out to the last detail, which received no more than a brief casual glance from the Jury. One of its members summarized the general view of this project by L-C and P.J.: "Lunatics", he said.

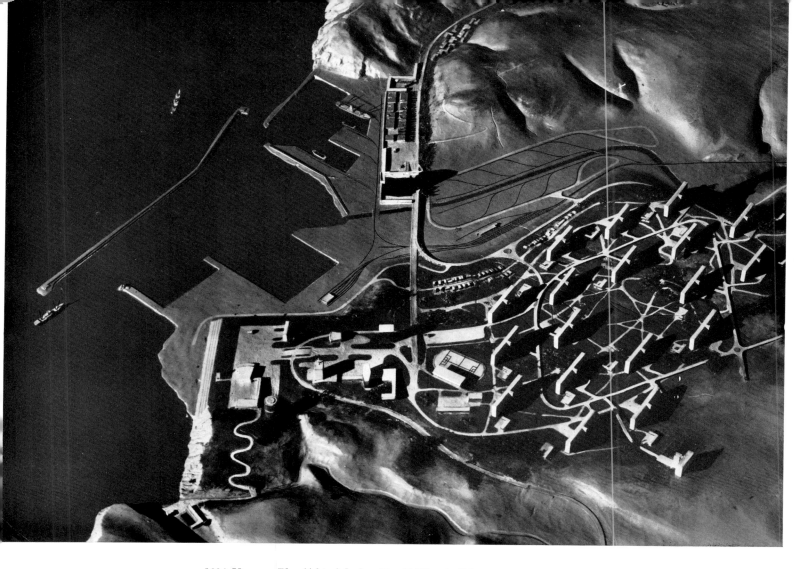

1934. Nemours Plan (Africa) declared by CIAM to be "the purest expression of the Athens Charter". The future town devised by L-C is the amphitheatre on the right. The wadi (watercourse), in the valley to the side, would be canalized, upstream, at a high level and diverted to irrigate the whole of the amphitheatre, which faces the sea. L-C sought the help of societies to buy the land, which was of no value at the time. Without success. In the end he was called upon by the municipality to defer his scheme. Nobody could understand that the place was suitable for accommodating 50,000 people .... The following year L-C was officially invited to visit the brothel which had just been built in the middle of this site, the first and only building to be seen .... It was Saturday; the ladies, in their petticoats and with handkerchiefs knotted about their perms, were scrubbing the cement floor of this paradise due to open its doors that evening.

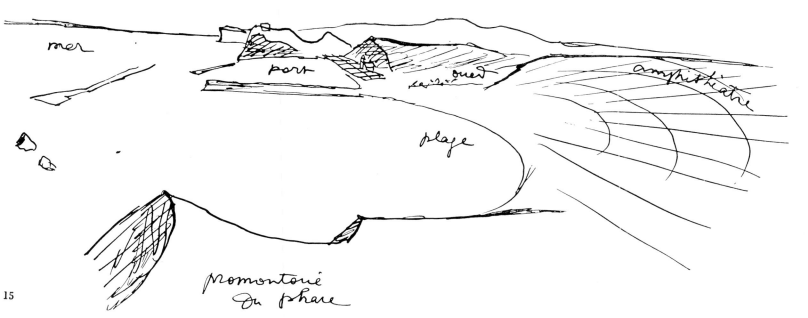

CET OUVRAGE EST DEDIE

a l **AUTORITÉ**

PARIS, MAI 1933

LE CORBUSIER

LA VILLE RADIEUSE

ELEMENTS D'UNE DOCTRINE D'URBANISME POUR L'EQUIPEMENT DE LA CIVILISATION MACHINISTE

PARIS
GENEVE
RIO DE JANEIRO
SAO PAOLO
MONTEVIDEO
BUENOS-AIRES
ALGER
MOSCOU
ANVERS
BARCELONE
STOCKHOLM
NEMOURS
PIACE

Les plans ne sont pas de la politique
Les plans sont le monument rationnel et lyrique
dressé au centre des contingences.
Les contingences sont le milieu : régions, races,
cultures, topographies, climats.
Ce sont, d'autre part, les ressources apportées
par les techniques modernes. Celles-ci
sont universelles
Les contingences ne doivent être évaluées qu'en
fonction de l'entité « homme », que par rapport à l'homme, que par rapport à nous.
à nous autres
une biologie
une psychologie

EDITIONS DE L'ARCHITECTURE D'AUJOURD'HUI

5, RUE BARTHOLDI, 5

BOULOGNE (Seine)

1935. BOOK

LA VILLE-RADIEUSE
(Collection de l'Equipement
de la Civilisation machiniste)

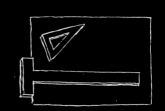

JE SUIS ATTIRÉ...

...Je suis attiré par toutes les organisations naturelles. Je ne puis fréquenter les salons; voici des années qu'on ne m'y a vu. Mais je m'aperçois que, fuyant la ville, je suis toujours là où sont des hommes en instance d'organisation. Je cherche les sauvages, non pour y trouver la barbarie, mais pour y mesurer la sagesse. Amérique ou Europe, paysans ou pêcheurs. Je comprends : je vais là où des hommes pratiquent des travaux servant à les nourrir et prennent des initiatives dont l'effet est d'alléger leur peine. Ils font aussi ce qu'il faut pour obtenir sans frais ni dépense, les joies de la sociabilité : métier, famille, collectivité. Je mesure donc qu'étant architecte et urbaniste, je viens apprendre les choses de mon métier chez *l'homme*, ou *chez les hommes*.

La ville? Mais c'est déjà du sous-produit. Le produit en sort, oui, mais exceptionnel et fini; c'est la qualité intense, le cristal. Fruit de la culture. Que de déchets, que de scories! Que de gênes, de malheurs, de niaiseries; que de gestes puérils, négateurs, destructeurs, d'ailleurs inconscients! Qu'apprendrions-nous dans un salon? Les cotes du jour? Et les potins? Et qu'y ferions-nous? Des échanges stériles d'incertitudes.

U.S.A. 1935. CONFERENCES

New York
Yale University, New Haven
Boston
Chicago
Madison
Philadelphia
Hartford
Vassar College
Columbia University, New York

1935. "La Ville Radieuse". A huge volume of plans and text, its contents designed to appeal to the "basic good sense of mankind".

PRÉLIMINAIRES

VACANCES 1932

LE PLAN : DICTATEUR

LIBERTÉ INDIVIDUELLE

PROPRIÉTÉ STÉRILE

OBJETS DE CONSOMMATION
STÉRILE

OBJETS DE CONSOMMATION
FÉCONDE

LIBERTÉ
ÉGALITÉ
FRATERNITÉ

ÉTAT DE CONSCIENCE MODERNE

1935. Polychromatic Sculpture. Louis Carré had borrowed L-C's studio for an exhibition entitled "Primitive Art": sculptures by Bénin, other negro sculptures, a few Greek, Henri Laurens, tapestries by Léger, paintings by Picasso, Braque and Le Corbusier. On the morning of the opening, a magnificent plaster cast had arrived in the studio from the Louvre, completely white and completely out of place. L-C said to Carré: "I don't want this pale thing here. Telephone the Louvre and ask them what colours would have been used originally on a splendid sculpture like this from the golden age of Greece." An hour later came the reply: "Sky blue, red ochre, white, and a dash or two of vermilion and green about the top of the head." Four pots of paint, but no brush. The palms of the hands would have to do. Two palms were pressed on the palette, steeped in colour and applied to the contours of the bust. In half an hour the trick was done. A poem in polychrome was the result, sparkling with life, brilliant. The palms, the thumbs, the finger tips had been enough to define the coloured surfaces to perfection; the sculpture had clearly been created for this. L-C commented: "It can never have been white."
(The tapestry at the back is Fernand Léger's; the sculpture in the foreground is by Henri Laurens.)

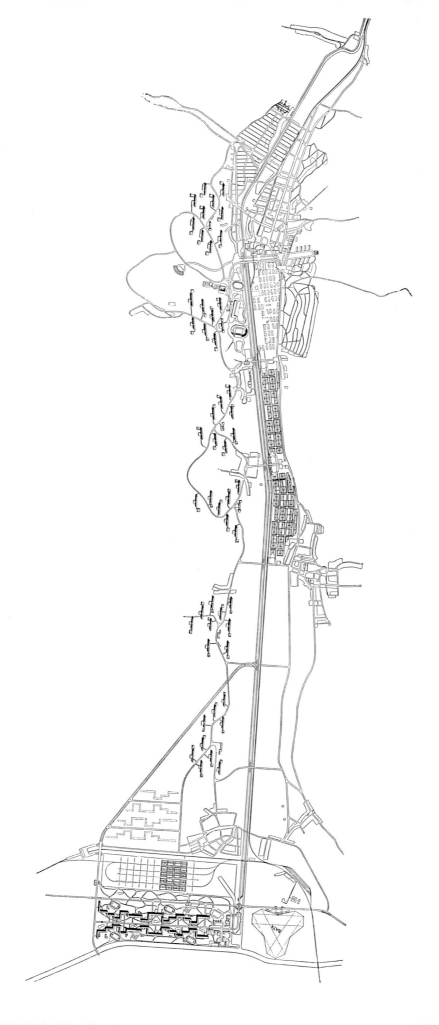

It was after this plan that
L-C set out on his first
journey to the U.S.A., and
wrote "*When the
Cathedrals were White*"....

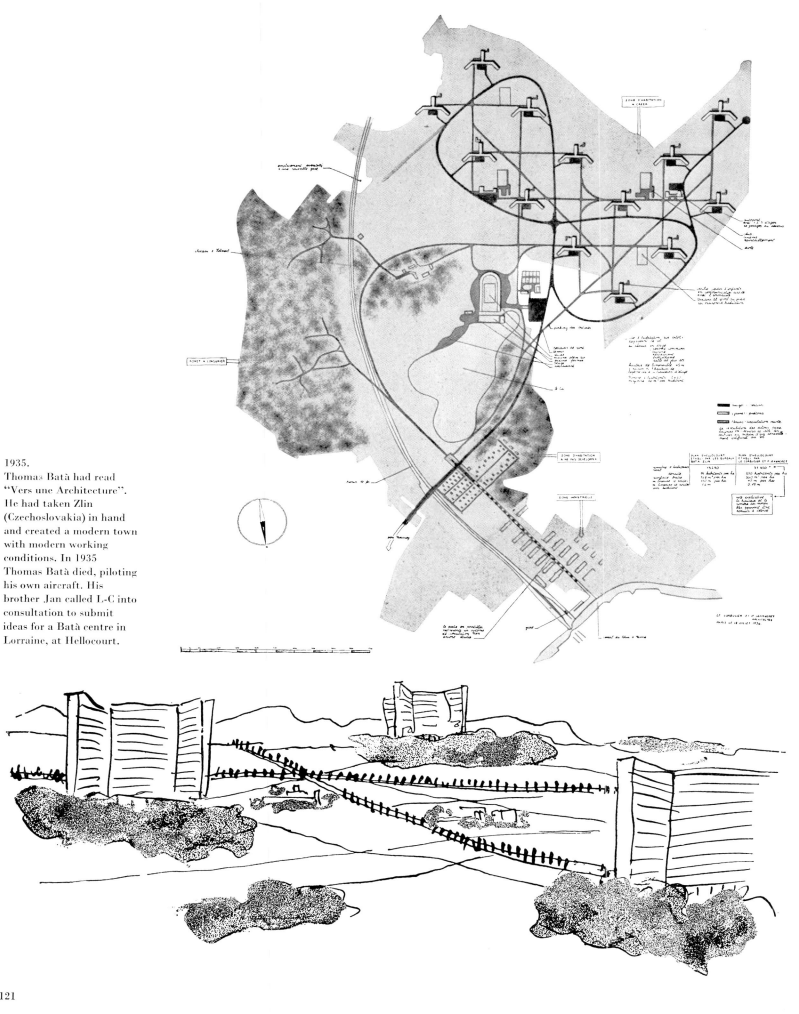

1935.
Thomas Batà had read
"Vers une Architecture".
He had taken Zlin
(Czechoslovakia) in hand
and created a modern town
with modern working
conditions. In 1935
Thomas Batà died, piloting
his own aircraft. His
brother Jan called L-C into
consultation to submit
ideas for a Batà centre in
Lorraine, at Hellocourt.

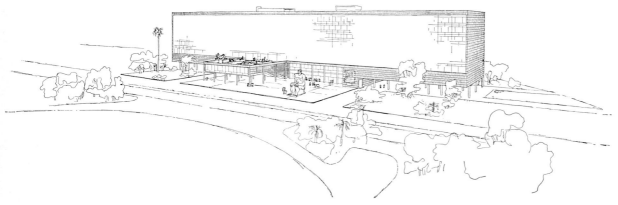

1936. At Lucio Costa's request, the Minister, Capanema, invited Le Corbusier to Rio to work in collaboration with Costa and his pupils on plans for the Ministry of Education. The site had been badly chosen and L-C looked about for another. On the eve of his departure, the Minister said to him: "Politics will prevent me from using this new site. What shall we do?" L-C replied: "Cut the office block vertically into two or three slabs and put them one on top of the other. At ground level leave things the same. Specify pink Rio granite for the whole of the site work and for the end walls, etc. ...." This the team did. One day the Minister said to L-C: "You have sited it all wrong, one of the two elevations faces north!...." (In the southern hemisphere the sun strikes the north side.) "That doesn't matter", said L-C, "we will fit brise-soleil!" (See note on page 111.)

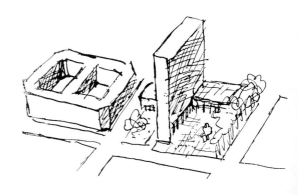

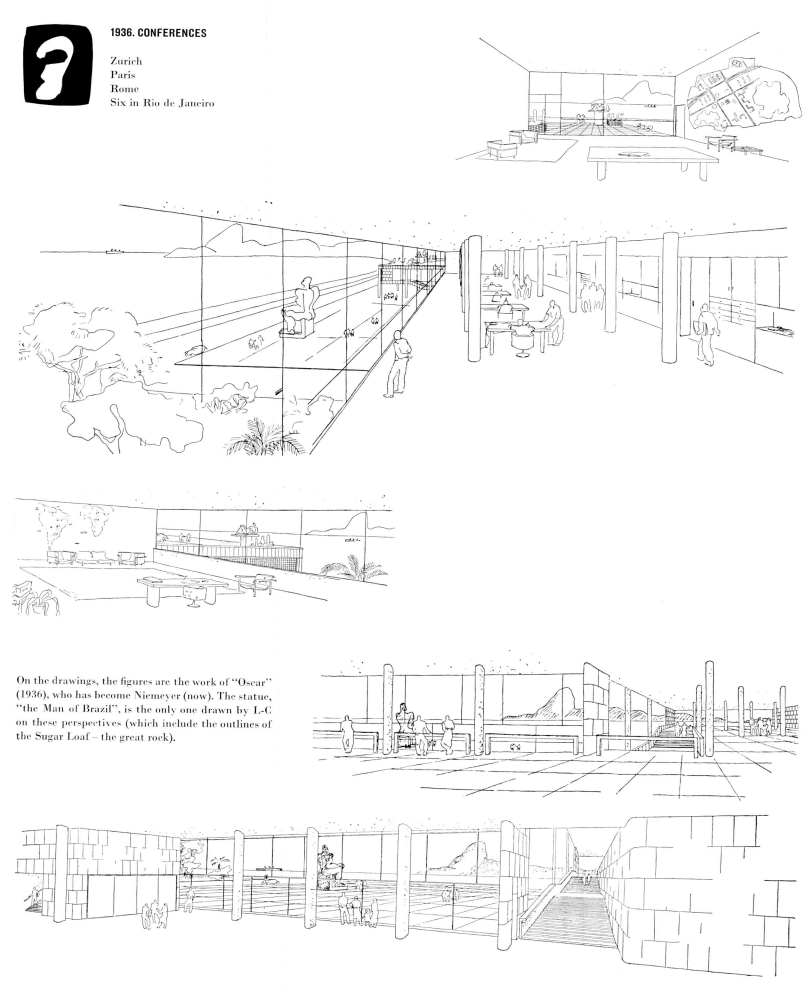

1936. CONFERENCES

Zurich
Paris
Rome
Six in Rio de Janeiro

On the drawings, the figures are the work of "Oscar" (1936), who has become Niemeyer (now). The statue, "the Man of Brazil", is the only one drawn by L-C on these perspectives (which include the outlines of the Sugar Loaf – the great rock).

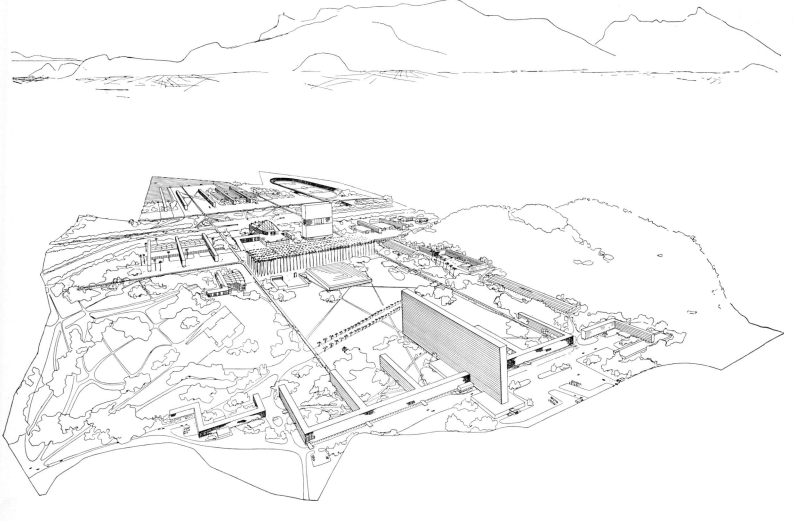

L-C's preliminary scheme for the University City of Brazil, 18 August 1936. A law of the land forbade the payment of a fee to a foreign architect. What was to be done? It was arranged that Le Corbusier should give six lectures at the theatre in Rio, and be paid as a "lecturer".

In the course of these lectures the public heard L-C's reactions, as a town-planner, to the landscape of Rio. He proposed something completely radical – a second town of unprecedented form, carried on pilotis 120 feet high with the lower groups of existing buildings radiating from each bay and passing beneath. And, 300 feet up, a level motorway 80 feet wide, linking all the hill tops, and creating order in the plan and townscape of Rio.   ⟶

recherche du passage
de l'autostrada cote 100 m.

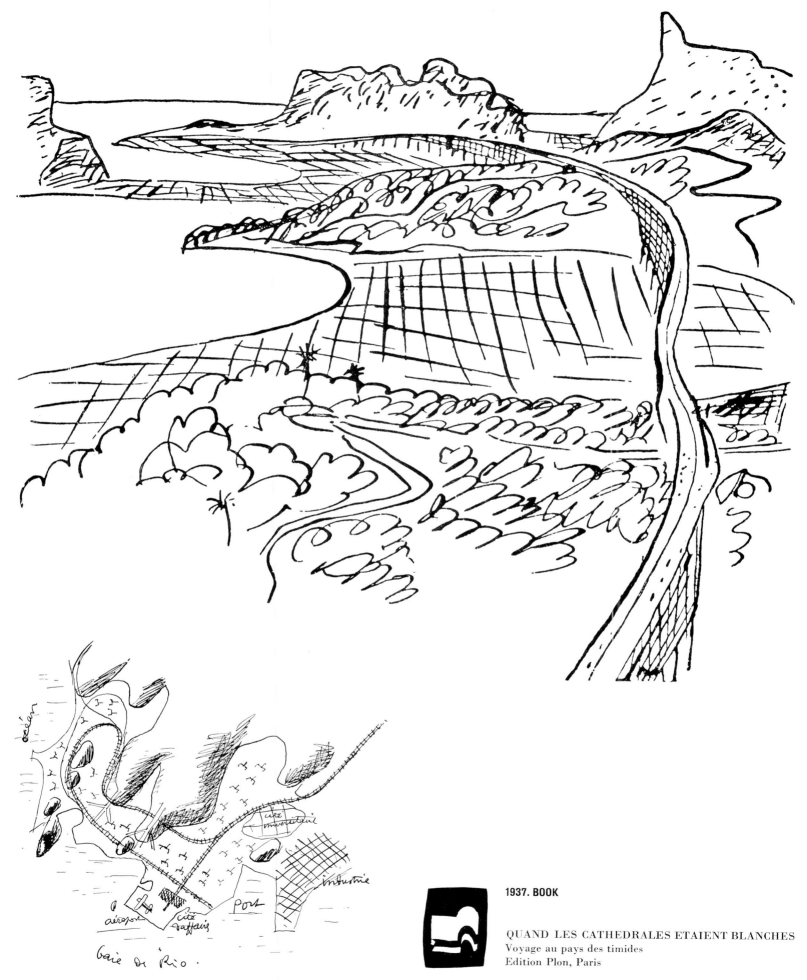

baie de Rio.

océan

cité universitaire

industrie

aéroport

Cité d'affaires

port

1937. BOOK

QUAND LES CATHEDRALES ETAIENT BLANCHES
Voyage au pays des timides
Edition Plon, Paris

125

re-formation cellulaire: le gratte-ciel

re-formation cellulaire: le logis

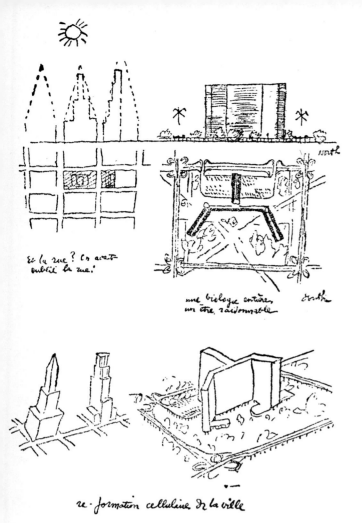

Et la rue? On avait oublié la rue!

une biologie entière: un être raisonnable

re-formation cellulaire de la ville

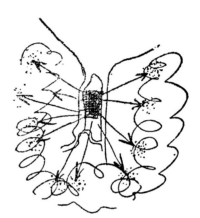

la Dislocation de la ville; naissance du cancer

1935. Journey to the U.S.A. L-C meets American skyscrapers. His reaction: "Your skyscrapers are too small, and there are too many." His proposal: "The Cartesian Skyscraper."

A study of the problem of adapting the present streets of New York to the new conditions created by the automobile.

An investigation (and proof) of the dislocation of metropolitan life by undue reliance on the garden-city concept. A prophecy (1935) about crucial points in Manhattan's future development, the significance of 42nd street, etc., etc., ...

Chronology: Paris 1922 (*"a city of 3 million inhabitants"*), Barcelona 1929, Rio 1929 and 1936, Buenos Aires 1929 and 1939, Algiers 1930 to 1942, Stockholm, Nemours, etc. .... And now, New York 1935 and a prophecy about the development of Manhattan; eleven years later (1946) the United Nations, Zeckendorf, Rockefeller (between 42nd and 47th streets) expressed L-C's ideas and took the credit for their country (the Wallace Harrisson incident).

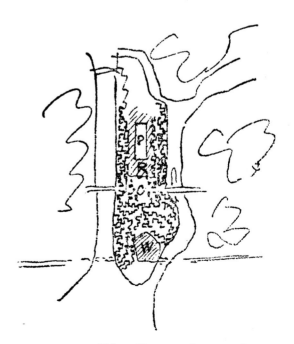

une nouvelle ville efficace in Manhattan: six million d'habitants

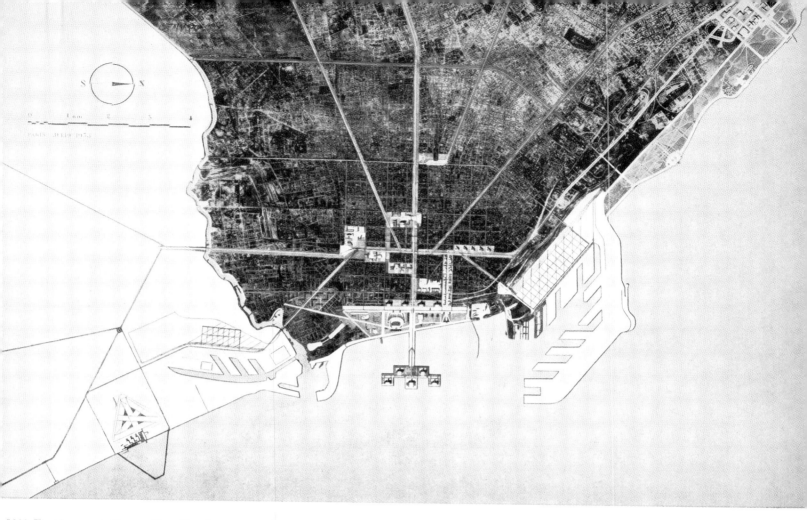

1929. First journey to Buenos Aires. The plans were made in Paris in 1939, transported in 1940 by miraculous contrivance over the roads of France during the débâcle of 1940 ...., and were laid at last on the table before the officially appointed committee in Buenos Aires (L-C was not there), when the Minister of Public Works observed: "If we invite Le Corbusier, it will mean that we are incapable of planning for ourselves ...." Thus the whole fate of the Buenos Aires plan was decided by the whim of a skilful speaker, while the committee sat quietly, impassively and democratically, by.

1938. BOOK

DES CANONS, DES MUNITIONS?
MERCI! DES LOGIS... S.V.P.
(Collection de l'Equipement
de la Civilisation machiniste)

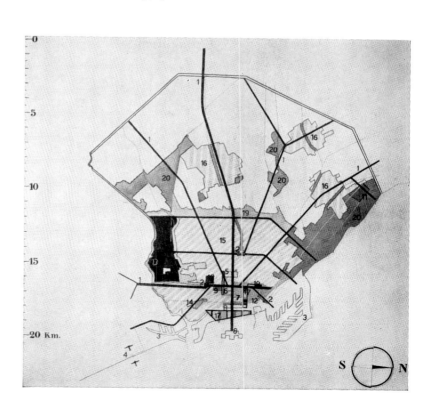

1937
EXPO. INT. DE L'HABITATION PARIS

LE PLAN

1

Nous ouvrons une rubrique permanente : « 1937 ». Nous avions, en 1924, institué déjà, au cours de douze numéros, une rubrique « 1925 : Expo. Art. Dec. Mod » (1). Ici, encore, nous nous plaçons hors de toutes personnalités et de toute polémique. Nous nous mettons au service de l'idée. Nous cherchons à servir. Nous nous abstenons de nous consacrer au cas des arts purs qui ont aujourd'hui, à leur disposition, dans le débat intellectuel, tous les moyens d'expression, d'exposition, d'attaque et de défense. Nous nous consacrons au cas poignant et des centaines et des centaines de milliers d'individus qui mènent une existence morne, tragique et sans espoir dans l'indifférence cruelle d'une vie urbaine demeurée sans plan. De ce point de vue hautement social, à l'occasion de l'Exposition internationale des Arts Modernes, prévue pour 1937, nous soumettons à l'opinion publique un plan.

NOTRE PLAN :

Nous proposons un autre titre à l'exposition annoncée :

1937
EXPOSITION INTERNATIONALE
DE L'HABITATION

(1) Voir l'Esprit nouveau N° 18 à 28 et dans la « Collection de l'Esprit Nouveau », Crès et Cie, le livre *L'Art décoratif d'aujourd'hui.*

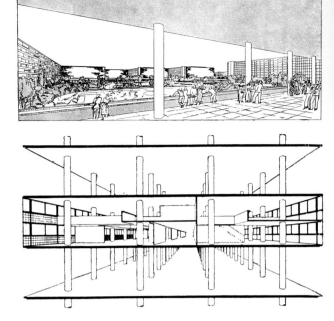

Competition of ideas (organized in 1932) for the theme of the coming International Exhibition in Paris of 1937. L-C's idea : change the title. Instead of an *"International Exhibition of Art and Technics"*, an *"International Exhibition of Housing"*. A site was suggested to the East of Paris; and then, instead of moving out completely into Eastern suburbia, *the proposal was to come back into Paris and initiate the great East-West throughway, which was completely lacking.* The formal framework of the exhibition was to be provided by an open stand, 150 feet high, which would make it possible to study, display and explain all the techniques, all the plans, all the equipment, and all the new ways of living. In short it was to be a comprehensive exposition of a problem which was already pressing, but which officialdom refused to consider : housing. In 1960 it has suddenly been noticed that Paris has 8 million inhabitants! Nobody knew it; nobody saw it happening; it was just allowed to occur.

L-C's proposals, 36 printed pages, did not even get a formal acknowledgment.

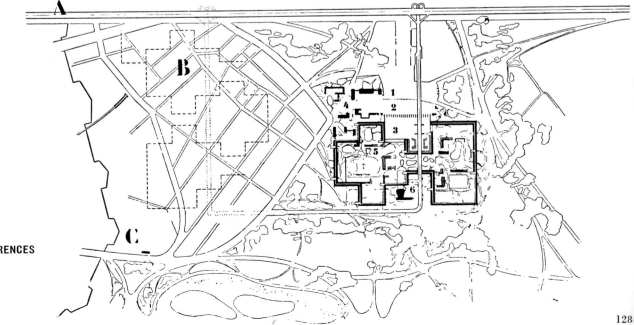

1937. CONFERENCES

Brussels
Lyons

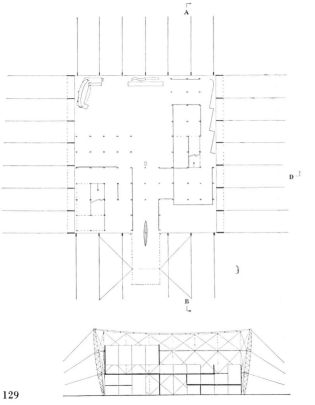

The result: a hushed silence! The whole exhibition was carried through without a single commission for L-C. The Prime Minister, Léon Blum, asked "What is Le Corbusier doing in the exhibition?" Answer: "Nothing at all." – "That's quite inconceivable." In December 1936, four months before the opening of the exhibition, the authorities offered thousands to L-C, if he would build. L-C replied that he didn't now want the money; that it was too late; that he had been refused the Kellerman bastion and that, in 1932, he had had no reply to his 1937 exhibition proposals. There was no site available anywhere, but L-C agreed to erect a tent with 17,000 sq.ft. of space for displaying every aspect of town-planning, both in its general application and with particular reference to Paris. The tent was put up in a few months. No bigwigs came to open it. It was the boldest thing you can imagine and contained the graphic features shown in the adjacent sketch.

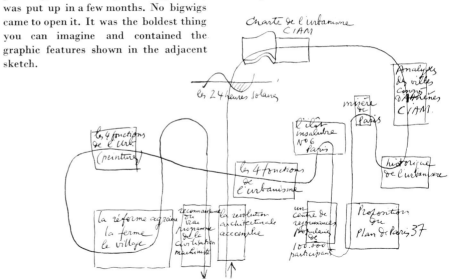

Paris Plan 1937, taken from "La Maison des Hommes (The Home of Man)". Located geographically between the hills of Paris. These two drawings form a conclusion and an affirmation.

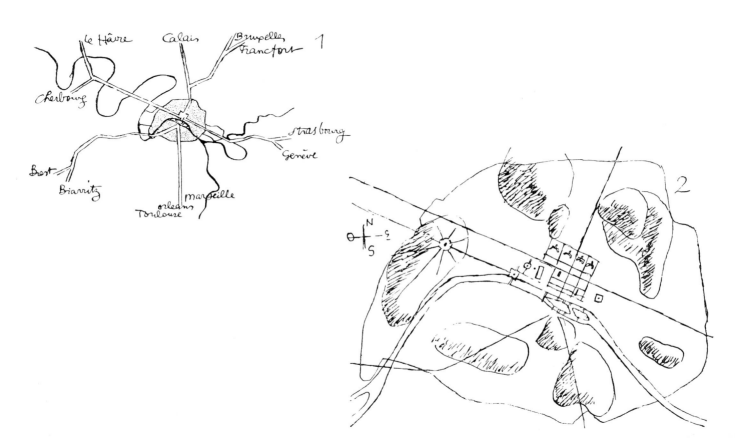

Here is the *Paris Plan 1937*. On the 6th January 1960 (twenty-three years later), the paper "ART", publishing these drawings, added this comment: "*A megalomania worse than Ledoux's, a vandalism unique in history, the dreary uniformity, vanity, and monotony of these skyscrapers .... have been proved spiritually and materially injurious, a contempt for historic and artistic tradition.*" (The author forgot to sign himself! ....)

1937. Stadium for 100,000 spectators (the first on such a scale to be worked out). L-C and P. J. show remarkable freedom and breadth of vision in handling a crowd of 100,000 people, a design which is the logical complement to olympic meetings and football matches, with provision also for open air theatre and cinema, public speeches, gymnastic exhibitions and, nowadays, electronic displays (as a result of the "Electronic Poem" of the Philips Pavilion, Brussels, 1958). In a word, a design which makes such enormous structures really come alive. Reaction: silence. This stadium offered solutions for the reception and dispersal of 100,000 people, which have never been matched since.

The Government of Irak were the first to show a practical interest, when, twenty years later, they commissioned their Sports Centre for Bagdad.

1939. One of seven mural paintings in a villa at Cap Martin (detail).

1939. Continuation of studies for the "Museum of Unlimited Expansion". Model prepared for Philippeville, Algeria (the Hitler war intervened). L-C has been building a museum like this at Ahmedabad, India, since 1952. Another at Tokyo for the Japanese government. Another still is projected for the Cultural Centre of Chandigarh. It has already been stated that a two-year study for the Porte Maillot, Paris, came to grief for .... very human reasons, only too human.

1939. CONFERENCE

Paris

Project for a monument to *Vaillant Couturier*. A competition had been organized by the Front Populaire in 1937–1938 for a monument to be placed at a junction of main roads converging on Paris. It would have been illuminated dramatically by the headlights of cars arriving at the road-fork, but it was rejected with a certain amount of nastiness. The most advanced artists, friends of L-C, castigated him for putting forward such a proposal. By the irony of events, at the Liberation after the Hitler War, the Museum of Modern Art of New York (Rockefeller) asked L-C what fee he would accept for a similar type of monument to American war veterans!!!

1939. September: war! Raoul Dautry, Minister of Munitions, commissioned L-C to build a cartridge-factory, the Moutiers-Rozeille plant, a 100% example of "L'Usine Verte" [key to the future *"Cités linéaires industrielles (linear industrial centres)"*] of the "3 ETABLISSEMENTS HUMAINS", 1942 and 1950. Then the collapse! A period in an abandoned farm at the foot of the Pyrenees. Pierre Jeanneret had from now on left the studio at 35 rue de Sèvres. Waiting and reflection. Painting was confined to preparations for pictures on typing paper. 1940: some gouaches, which will appear later – potential patterns for sculpture. Savina, a Breton cabinet-maker and wood-sculptor, made bold statues from them in timber. During the Occupation, L-C, with no private or public commissions of any kind, published "Sur les 4 Routes", "Destin de Paris", "La Maison des Hommes", the text of the latter book being written by François de Pierrefeu, and "La Charte d'Athènes" (not under L-C's name, but with an introductory piece by Jean Giraudoux). In 1943, L-C founded the ASCORAL (Assemblée de Constructeurs pour une Rénovation architecturale). Eleven sections and sub-sections, each bringing together four to ten people representing every branch of activity and all ages. Each section met twice a month. L-C thus presided over 22 committees a month for a year. These sections were: (1) General ideas and co-ordination; (2) The art of (modern) living (a subject for teaching in schools); (3) Standardization in the building field, (a) Domestic equipment, (b) Home construction, (c) Industrialization of the home; (4) Hygiene; (5) Work, (a) Agriculture, (b) Industry; (6) Folklore (study of traditions); (7) Finance and legislation; (8) The business side. Two lines added to this catalogue of sections appear significant to-day. They were: *"The whole conception (of the Ascoral) is based upon the home considered as a centre of planning problems."* The meetings of the Ascoral took place at various places in Paris, and particularly in the studio at 35 rue de Sèvres, which had been ransacked and abandoned to dust.

Liberation: Raoul Dautry, the first Minister of Reconstruction, said to L-C in 1945: "Which town are you reconstructing?" "None!" "What building are you reconstructing? Nothing? Well, La Rochelle is still occupied and we think the German army will blow it up as they retire. Would you like to do the plan for La Rochelle-Pallice?" (La Pallice is the deep water harbour adjoining La Rochelle.) At the same time industrialists of much damaged St. Dié (Vosges) commissioned L-C to prepare a plan for their town. The plans for St. Dié and La Rochelle, with Nemours d'Afrique, express more eloquently than any other the researches of L-C and represent the very spirit of the Athens Charter. These plans were not approved by the gentleman responsible for town-planning in France for fifteen years! Officially L-C is still chief planning consultant for La Rochelle, but he has not been consulted since 1947, nor paid (13 years) .... The plan for St. Dié, accepted by Americans as "evidence of a French renaissance", was shown in travelling exhibitions in towns throughout the USA and Canada.

1946; L-C was sent to New York by the French government, as delegate to the "site commission" (nine members from all countries) for UNO to defend modern architecture and town design in a problem of world importance. In New York L-C was stupefied, flabbergasted, by the discussions, and activities of this commission. By the

1939—1941. BOOK

SUR LES 4 ROUTES
Editions de la N.R.F.

137

sixth week he had left it, declaring "I am returning to Paris, but I will let you have *a minority report* beforehand." The chairman of the commission (an Englishman) inquired: "Who is this fanatical fellow inflicted upon us by France?" A few days later Mr. Noel-Baker said to this chairman, "Ah, you've got Mr. Le Corbusier, have you? He's a grand person" – and L-C returned to the struggle in New York for five more months. His minority report ("Report by the Delegate of France") landed like a bomb in front of the Assembly General of UNO, when it appeared as Appendix I to the memorandum of the "Commission of 54 nations". "Worthy of Montaigne!" declared His Excellency Zuleta, Minister from Colombia, who presided over this big commission .... In the eighth month the Assembly of UNO decided to acquire the 42nd Street site by the East River, New York, thus confirming L-C's contentions. But, pay careful attention! In the only speech made by L-C to the 54-nation commission, he asserted, "If you have a sense of humour .... don't forget that the site adopted to-day is 1,500 times smaller *than the one claimed by your commission! ....*" Three weeks later UNO showed its confidence in L-C by appointing him one of the experts on the new commission for the construction of the UN building overlooking the East River. L-C drew up the plans, directing the team of draughtsmen in the RKO Building (New York, Rockefeller Center) .... from the 25th January to the end of June 1947 (five months) .... Then came the most appalling shock that a man could suffer – a shock to fundamental human decency, to friendship itself. (The perceptive reader will know what I mean!)

Pourtant, devant l'opinion mondiale, cette attribution unitaire, dictée par la confiance de l'U.S.A. en son propre destin, et le désir de M Trygve-Lie d'aller vite, installent un dilemme pertinent entre la force et le droit, droit moral, élevé, morale du droit, morale simple. Les arguments juridiques, peuvent sembler substantiels; mais se dresse en travers la notion pure et simple de l'honnêteté fondamentale. Arguments de business ou valeur spirituelle? That is the question! **l'Honnêteté fondamentale.** Paris, février 1948.

But in 1945, Raoul Dautry, Minister of Reconstruction, entered into an agreement with Le Corbusier for the erection at Marseilles of an "Unité d'Habitation de Grandeur Conforme". L-C accepted on condition that any regulations in force at the time would be relaxed in his favour. This was granted, and it was, therefore, possible to build the "Unité de Marseille". Five years of storm, spite and uproar followed, despicable, ugly. A hue and cry by the press. Claudius Petit, who succeeded as minister, showed his courage by taking L-C's part. When the "Unité" was finished on the Boulevard Michelet, a case for 20 million francs in damages was brought against L-C for disfiguring the French landscape: an old gentleman of 80, entirely unknown, was the plaintiff, president of a society (equally obscure) for the "preservation of the French countryside" .... The case was lost by the society and the old gentleman, and suddenly the people of Marseilles turned a favourable eye upon what had been its shame and embarrassment for five years: the "Unité" was spontaneously christened "Le Corbusier", and painted signboards bearing the same legend now point the way to the place from all over the town. A bank was granted the concession rights for showing visitors round the building, and proceeded to pocket with the State 30 million francs without disgorging a penny for the money-box of the studio draughtsmen at 35 rue de

Sèvres .... "L' Unité de Marseille" has become a place of pilgrimage for students from every country. A co-operative team of workers built the second "Unité" of Nantes-Rezé; a third was constructed at Berlin at the request of the German government on the finest site in the city: the olympic hill. Alas, a financier and two acquiescent German architects changed the plans behind the scenes and had mass-produced components prefabricated without L-C's knowledge. According to the financier "– properties of this sort are unsuitable for children. We shall only provide homes for single people and childless couples" .... Sensational nonsense! Disloyalty and idiocy combined. The fourth "Unité" is now being completed at Briey-en-Forêt, amid the woods and birdsong of Lorraine. Five new "Unités" are to be built at Meaux, thanks to exceptional production methods! The tenth "Unité", in open country, will dominate the town of Firminy (where Claudius Petit is mayor) .... and this is the theory upon which the "Unités d'Habitation de Grandeur Conforme" is based: *If you want to bring up your family in the peace and seclusion of a real home, in "natural conditions"* (sun, space, greenery), form groups of 2,000 people (men, women and children); go in by a single door; take the four lifts (20 people to each) which serve the eight, superimposed, internal streets. You will then be alone, you will meet no one, you will be in peace, sunlight and space, and the green world outside will stream in through your windows. Your children will play on the grass and in a roof garden ....
In 1950, or thereabouts, the President of the Association of Doctors of the Seine (department) had been filling the French press with scares of this sort: "Le Corbusier will unleash a mass of lunatics over France by the uproar and confusion" (which he advocates). In Marseilles the representative of the Ministry of Town-planning joined in the chorus of alarm. A year later .... (peace and seclusion having been demonstrated in practice), he was deploring *"the tragic loneliness"* ....
1953. Triumphant opening of the "Unité de Marseille" by the Minister, Claudius Petit. The official photographs of the ceremony show Le Corbusier's bitter opponent from the Mayor's offices in Marseilles, wreathed in smiles at L-C's side. The facts can be verified!
1948. Pierre Beaudouin came forward to help L-C in trying his hand at tapestry. With extraordinary patience and in face of obstruction from certain officials, Beaudouin succeeded in inspiring the weavers at Aubusson. Enthusiastic optimism. The tapestries, woven in quantity, were baptized by L-C "Muralnomad", which means that, in this age of the revival of mural painting, tapestry fulfils the same aspirations, follows the same ideas and performs the same functions. But in this case the wall is of wool, ... for modern man has become a nomad living in building with communal services. We are talking about tapestries at least 7 feet 3 inches high and, as a general rule, touching the ground, with an approximate width of 7 ft. 5 in., 9 ft. 8 in., 12 ft., 15 ft. 6 in., etc. ....
The "woollen" wall can also serve an acoustic purpose under certain circumstances. In 1956 Le Corbusier had woven in cashmere, to his own designs, 7,000 sq. ft. of tapestry for the Chief Justice's Chamber (this tapestry was 1,500 sq. ft. alone) and for the eight other rooms (eight tapestries, each 700 sq. ft.) of the High Court building at Chandigarh in India. In Tokyo, Sakakura (at one time an architect at 35 rue de Sèvres) has hung a 2,000 square-foot tapestry, signed Le Corbusier, in the auditorium of his new theatre – a dynamic surface feature, and deliberately the only one.
In November 1950 two men came to 35 rue de Sèvres to talk to Le Corbusier about the new capital of the Punjab (India), which they were proposing to build: P. N. Thapar, Secretary to the Punjab Government Capital Project, and P. L. Varma, Chief Engineer of the Punjab. Thapar had been responsible for the legal instrument (it was just a little "Oxfordish" perhaps), while Varma had sought, and found, a site for the town. He chose with care and then took an enormous responsibility which has conferred on his country an inestimable benefit. These

two men have created a capital: they were ordinary civil servants, but their decisions were worthy of statesmen. Mr. Nehru came to see Chandigarh and showed his confidence in L-C. They understood each other. He has guided Le Corbusier round dangerous corners. For nine years there have been ties of friendship and mutual esteem between the Man of India and L-C. Chandigarh is not, as it might have been, a sudden, dazzling, efflorescence of a tropical flower. It is a contribution adjusted to human scale – to human size and dignity – by the efforts of a few men of character, worn, chafed and buffeted by the shocks and frictions of human relations, by the clash of individual personalities and temperaments. So be it! There is a debit and a credit side to every enterprise. Let us look at the credit side ....

1951. L-C found himself the prospective architect for UNESCO. The favoured prospect, too, it seemed. He had written a letter on the 23rd July 1951 to Mr. Torres Bodet, the Director General. When Mr. Carneiro (Brazil) proposed in a plenary session of the Commission the unconditional nomination of Le Corbusier, the USA interposed a veto (the first). The very next day the ambassador of the United States in Paris, at a public ceremony at the Embassy, conferred on L-C the title of Honorary Member of the National Institute of Arts and Letters of New York. His concluding words: "Well, Mr. Le Corbusier, as you yourself have written somewhere, the time has come for tackling the big jobs! ..." "Forgive me, Mr. Ambassador, but only yesterday your government vetoed my participation in the UNESCO scheme!"

Two others voted against the two proposals of the *Committee of 5 Experts,* of which Le Corbusier had been the first to be nominated (on the recommendation of Carneiro, Brazil) and of which he had been asked to nominate the four other members: Walter Gropius, Lucio Costa, Markelius and Rogers. In all five eminent members of CIAM (Germany, Brazil, Sweden, Italy, France) were thus empowered to guide the architects and engineer who were then appointed. These two new proposals reflected the confidence of the Committee of Five in L-C.

1951. The plans for the city of Bogotá were a consequence of the friendly regard which had existed between L-C and His Excellency Zuleta, since the latter's intervention at UNO in 1946.

Ronchamp and the Monastery of La Tourette have been built for deeply human reasons: the adoration of the Virgin for Ronchamp, and the spartan life of the preaching friars for La Tourette. The human scale of heart and body, living human clay – and an unexpected episode. Once in the past L-C had said, "I want to reintroduce the temple to the home and *make the home the temple of the family"*, which meant the intention to render family life sacred, to give it a setting at once splendid and practical. Ronchamp and La Tourette have become like Marseilles (L'Unité d'Habitation) stages in a pilgrimage which started from many different points.

1951. *"La Règle des 7 V. qui sont 8"* (The Rule of the 7 Vs) was laid down at the request of one of the offices of Unesco. It dictated the town plan of Chandigarh .... as it did the "South Marseilles" plan (10 sq. miles) in 1951. This was a plan ordered by a minister, adopted by a minister and declared "never received!" by the relevant official.

Meantime, the city of Algiers had decided on its plan and work had been started .... by others.

Bagdad had asked Le Corbusier for plans for its sports centre on the banks of the Tigris.

In Tokyo the Japanese government called in Le Corbusier to erect a cultural centre to contain the "Museum of Western Modern Art" (Matsukata Collection). But L-C added a museum for temporary exhibitions and another for new collections.

About 1954 "La Grille Climatique (climatic grid)" was worked out in Le Corbusier's studio. L-C was overwhelmed and discouraged by the uncertainties enveloping the complex effects of the sun in tropical countries.

But he had also gone into the question of difficulties in solutions to building problems in temperate zones, since the sensational innovations of the "plan libre", glass wall, etc. .... The duel of earth and sun, of latitude and the axis of the earth with the sun's orbit.

Instead of an idiotic hocus-pocus confusion of popular traditional methods, the climatic grid sets out the problem of the sun for every differing occasion.

1959. The people of Harvard-Cambridge-Boston-U.S.A. made a charming gesture to L-C, inviting him to build, in the heart of the old University, a house in which it will be possible to bring into existence a true union of head and hand; in which time will not be the supreme regulating factor. This, in a country and age which inspired that insult to mankind "Time is money!".

In 1956 L-C was asked to accept membership of the Institut de France (Académie des Beaux-Arts) in Paris: "Thank you, never! .... My name would serve as a banner to conceal the present evolution of the Ecole des Beaux-Arts towards a superficial modernism" .... Le Corbusier is a member (against his will) of every academy in the world; one gets nominated to such places without being asked. But Paris is something altogether graver, more serious, more involved. There are times when one's moral responsibility to others ....

The housing catastrophe grows in France. In thirty years L-C has not built a single dwelling in Paris. Yet he has carried further than ever his minutely detailed studies of the problem, to the ultimate pinnacle, indeed, of industrial technique. Tireless, undismayed, confident that his mission will succeed .... Alas for Paris, the wasteland, the ruthless battlefield! One day the crust of your harsh earth will yield, and roots will spring .... those roots of Paris, great mute city, secret and supreme ....

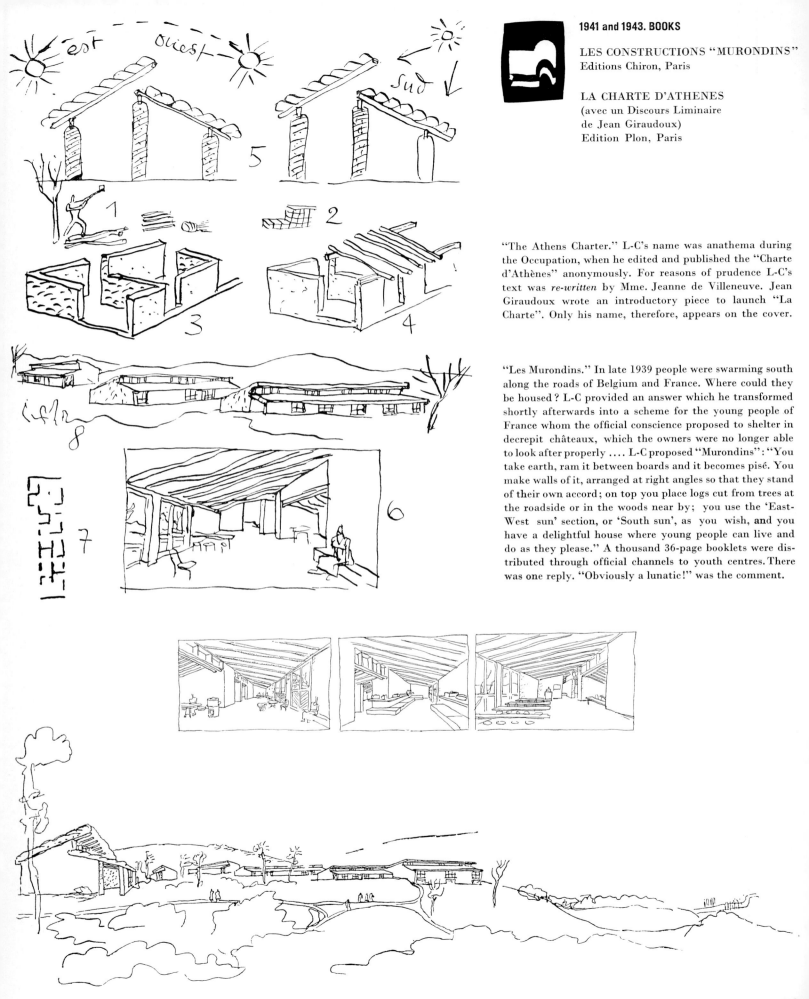

LES CONSTRUCTIONS "MURONDINS"
Editions Chiron, Paris

LA CHARTE D'ATHÈNES
(avec un Discours Liminaire
de Jean Giraudoux)
Edition Plon, Paris

"The Athens Charter." L-C's name was anathema during the Occupation, when he edited and published the "Charte d'Athènes" anonymously. For reasons of prudence L-C's text was *re-written* by Mme. Jeanne de Villeneuve. Jean Giraudoux wrote an introductory piece to launch "La Charte". Only his name, therefore, appears on the cover.

"Les Murondins." In late 1939 people were swarming south along the roads of Belgium and France. Where could they be housed ? L-C provided an answer which he transformed shortly afterwards into a scheme for the young people of France whom the official conscience proposed to shelter in decrepit châteaux, which the owners were no longer able to look after properly .... L-C proposed "Murondins": "You take earth, ram it between boards and it becomes pisé. You make walls of it, arranged at right angles so that they stand of their own accord; on top you place logs cut from trees at the roadside or in the woods near by; you use the 'East-West sun' section, or 'South sun', as you wish, and you have a delightful house where young people can live and do as they please." A thousand 36-page booklets were distributed through official channels to youth centres. There was one reply. "Obviously a lunatic !" was the comment.

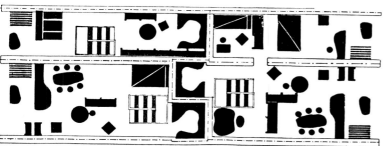

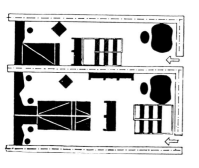

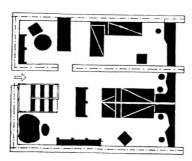

Houses called "Mesopotamians", so called by L-C in the jargon of 35 rue de Sèvres, to describe mass-produced house types, as the archaeologists show them in their books, in Mesopotamia or elsewhere. Representing a basically "human" tradition and respected by the intellectuals, because it was Babylonian. But hated by municipal officialdom at La Rochelle. Copy the corinthian orders or what-have-you to build town halls, why certainly! But harness the wisdom of the ancients to house crowds of evacuees, never!

These "Mesopotamians", in comparison with what was built officially, were "radiant homes".

Soltan, from L-C's studio, was almost thrown out of the mayor's office at La Rochelle for rashly using the term "Mesopotamian". "You are in France, Sir!" "Thank you, Mr. Mayor."

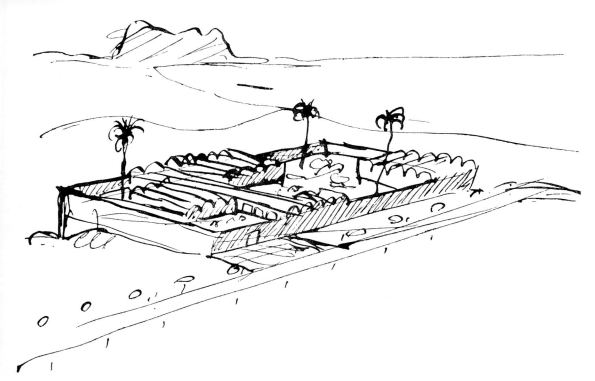

Study for smallholders' ("colons") homes in Algeria. The problem was not to "colonise", but to provide accommodation suitable to the climate and to local conditions.

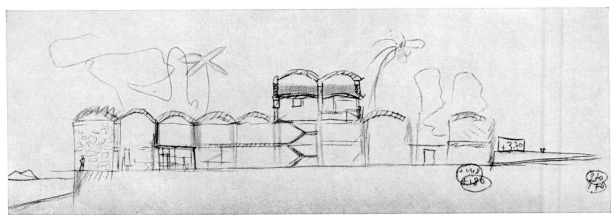

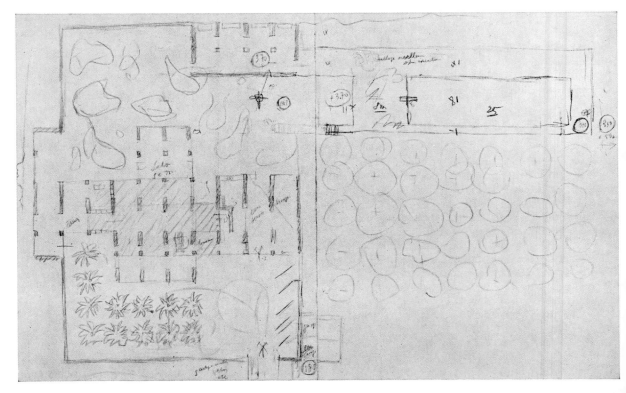

During the Occupation – the Pyrenean oil affair. L-C, with a colleague, was secretly instructed to hold himself in readiness for planning and architectural work in the Pyrenees. A fat report on planning in the Pyrenees, by him, still exists somewhere in the archives of the Ministry (1943). It is divided into Agriculture, Industrialization, tourism. L-C witnessed the first "gushers" not far from Saint-Gaudens. He envisaged a possible future development of the town as a separate entity, with an industrial centre outside. After 1946: good-bye, Mr. Corbu! ....

ASCORAL
Assemblée
de Constructeurs
pour une
Rénovation
Architecturale

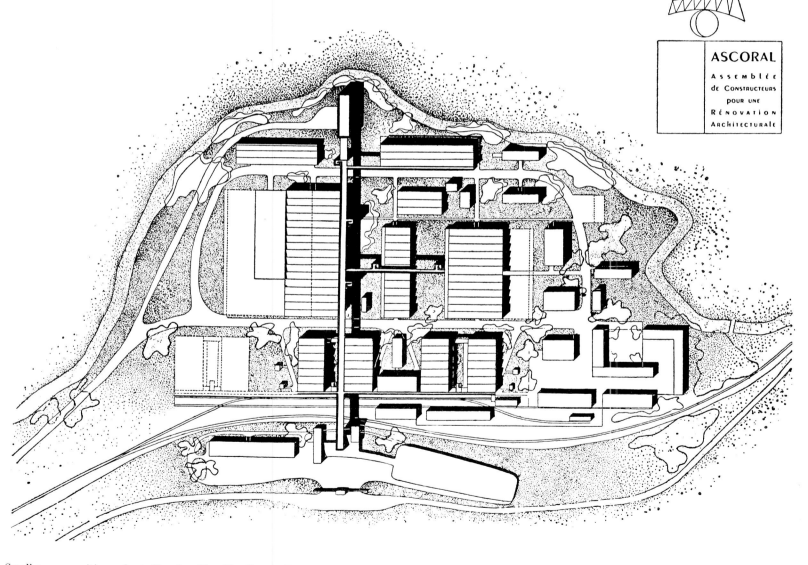

Small-arms munitions plant, Moutiers-Rozeille, Creuse. Prototype of the "Usine Verte (Green factory)", key to the "Linear Industrial centre" which emerged from the work of the ASCORAL.
Colonel: "It has never been possible to manufacture cartridges by production-line methods." "All the same, Colonel, let me take charge of the production-line." L-C's methods solved the problem. The Minister of Munitions, M. Dautry, ordered site work to begin immediately. He ordered a second factory in Algeria. "It's for the war", thought Corbu, "It's bound to be built!" Disaster. The foundations were soon lost in undergrowth, so the farmer went to work instead.

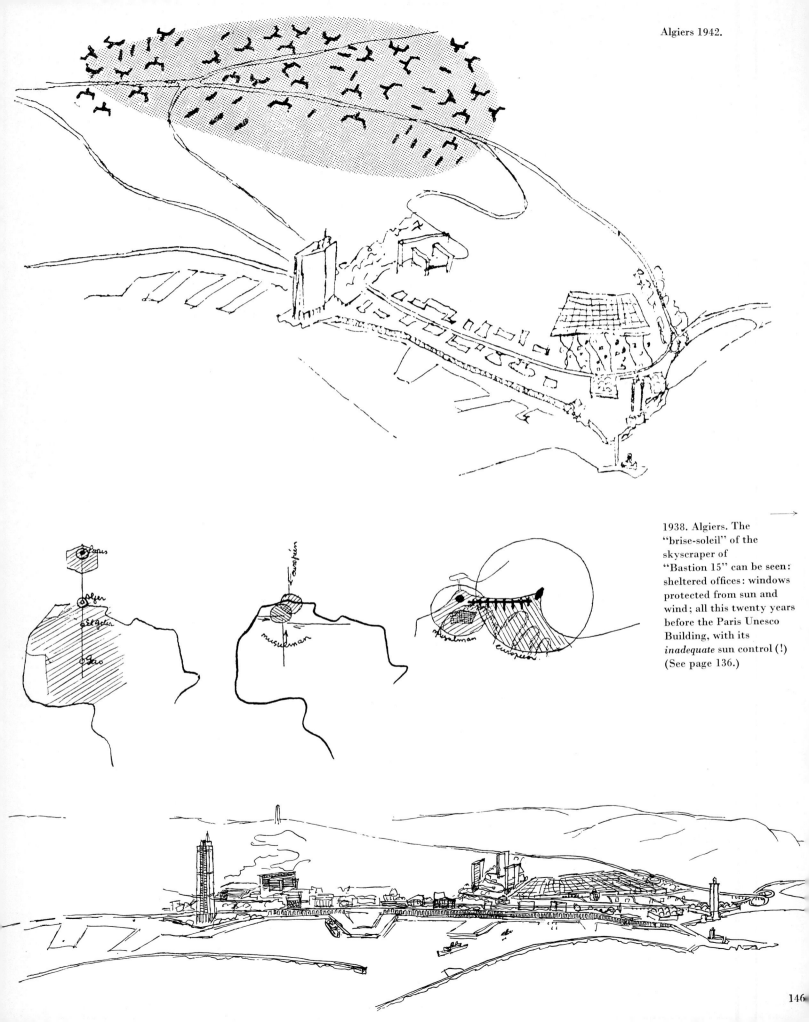

Algiers 1942.

1938. Algiers. The "brise-soleil" of the skyscraper of "Bastion 15" can be seen: sheltered offices: windows protected from sun and wind; all this twenty years before the Paris Unesco Building, with its *inadequate* sun control (!) (See page 136.)

146

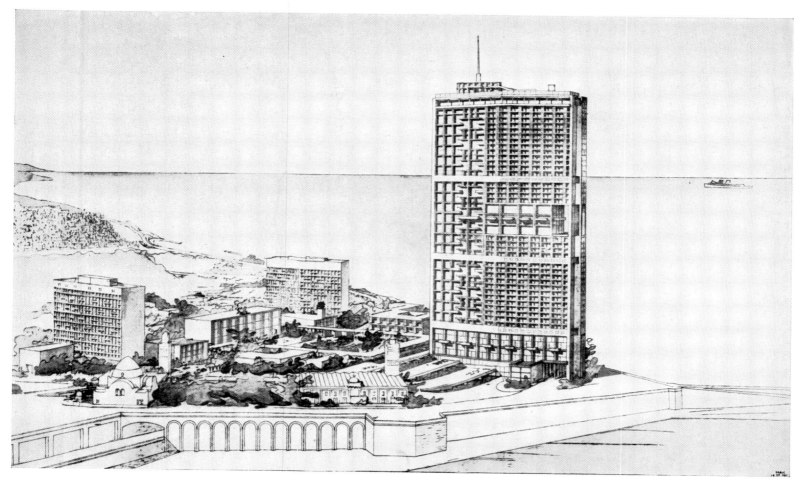

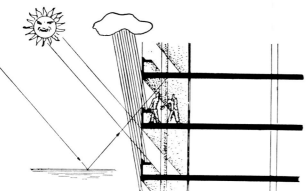

L-C in Algiers, twelve years of study, often on the spot. Twelve eventful years of architecture and town-planning. The final project proposed a Commercial Centre on Bastion 15, on the left, to preserve the Casbah, a masterpiece of historic town design. Nothing would be demolished, but on the heights of Mustapha open sites would be found for a residential "Ville-Radieuse" (various types of "Unités d'Habitation", 160 feet high, with views in every direction: North, East, South and West – the sea to the North; the range of the Atlas to the South ....)

In 1942 the Municipal Council, declaring that L-C was ruining the entire city, rejected the scheme. The culmination of twelve years work and the way to an amicable "Musulman-European" society: looked at panoramically, the Moslem citadel and the Casbah on the Cap de la Marine; on Bastion 15, the Commercial centre, and between the two every possible means of access to the port.

Town-planning expresses the life of an era. Architecture reveals its spirit. Some men have original ideas and are kicked on the behind for their pains.

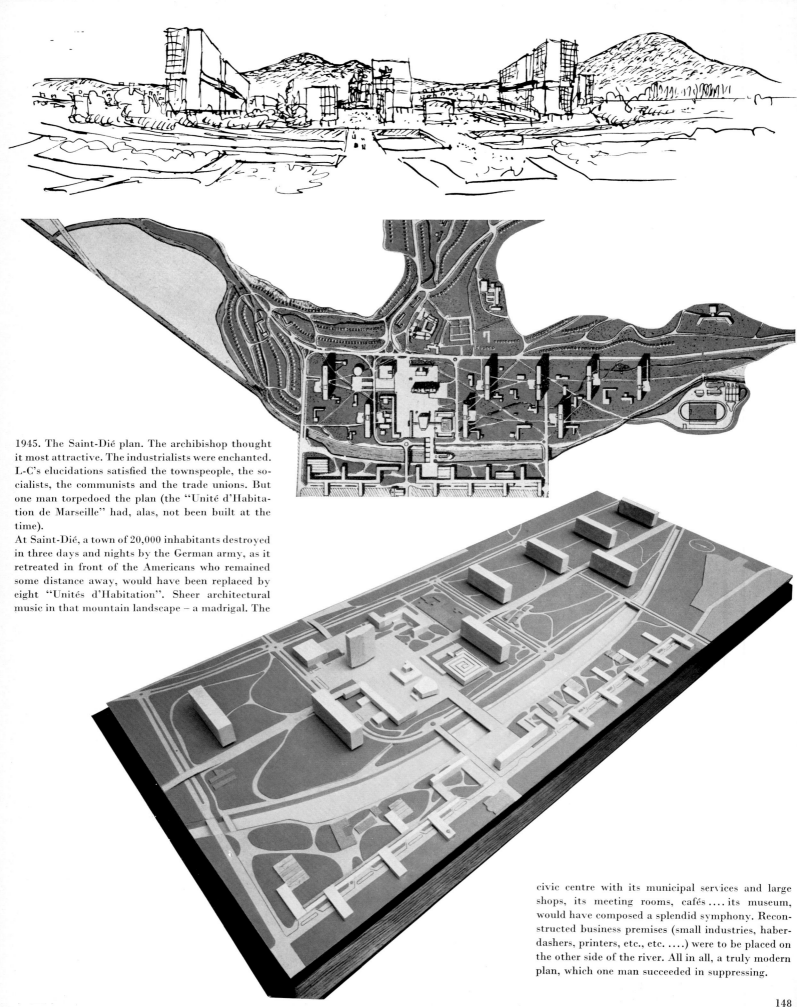

1945. The Saint-Dié plan. The archibishop thought it most attractive. The industrialists were enchanted. L-C's elucidations satisfied the townspeople, the socialists, the communists and the trade unions. But one man torpedoed the plan (the "Unité d'Habitation de Marseille" had, alas, not been built at the time).

At Saint-Dié, a town of 20,000 inhabitants destroyed in three days and nights by the German army, as it retreated in front of the Americans who remained some distance away, would have been replaced by eight "Unités d'Habitation". Sheer architectural music in that mountain landscape – a madrigal. The civic centre with its municipal services and large shops, its meeting rooms, cafés .... its museum, would have composed a splendid symphony. Reconstructed business premises (small industries, haberdashers, printers, etc., etc. ....) were to be placed on the other side of the river. All in all, a truly modern plan, which one man succeeded in suppressing.

1945–46. Plan for La Rochelle-Pallice. By a miracle the town was not destroyed, the two opposing commanders recognizing one another as one-time fellow students at Strasbourg University. So the guns were silenced when the German retreat started, and the town of La Rochelle was saved from destruction. But the plan proceeded. It entailed linking the small fishing port at the end of a natural gulf with a free, deep-water, port facing the open sea: the port of La Pallice. A demonstration of town-planning in action: 1) protection for historic monuments (the port and town of La Rochelle); 2) creation of a free port: the port of La Pallice; 3) a modern residential town with 10 "Unités d'Habitation", 20,000 inhabitants, etc. . . . right in the country, with sun, space, green fields and recreation at one's door step. The plan was sabotaged under the same conditions as the one for Saint-Dié.

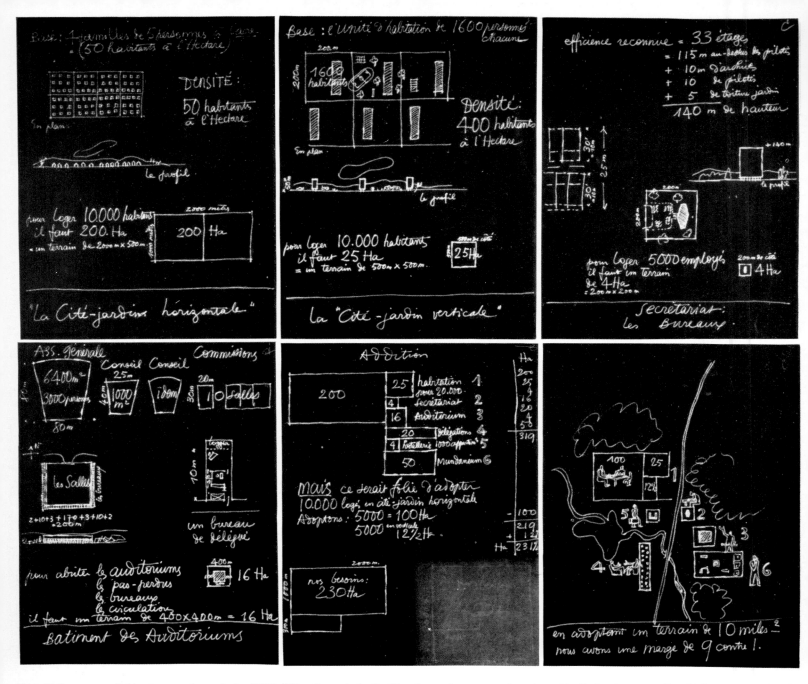

1946. L-C was one of the nine members of the UNO "Site Commission". The plates above are taken from his "minority report", which was immediately made public by the book "U.N. Headquarters".

1945 and 1947. BOOKS

MANIERE DE PENSER L'URBANISME
(ASCORAL)
Editions l'Architecture d'Aujourd'hui,
Boulogne s. S.

U.N. HEADQUARTERS
Reinhold Publishing Corp., New York

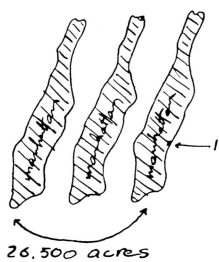

17 acres

26,500 acres

Site proposed by the "Commission": 26,500 acres (= three times the area of Manhattan); site acquired in the end by the United Nations: 17 acres (fifteen hundred times less).

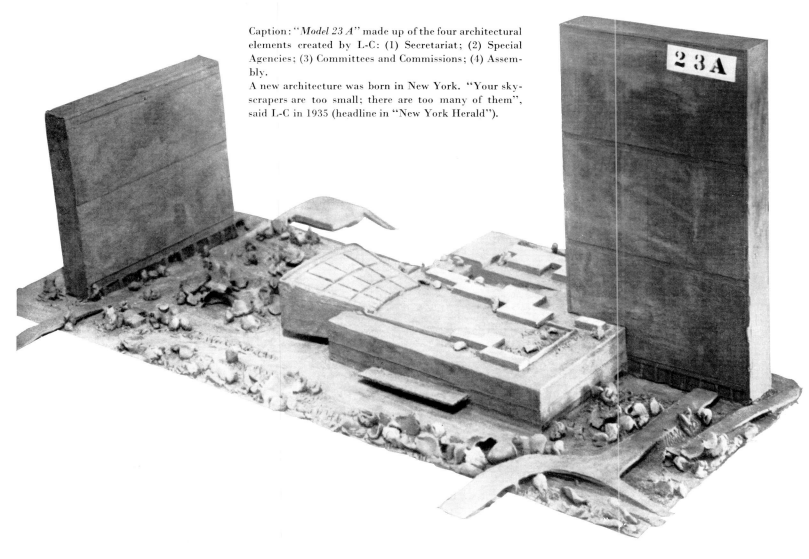

Caption: *"Model 23 A"* made up of the four architectural elements created by L-C: (1) Secretariat; (2) Special Agencies; (3) Committees and Commissions; (4) Assembly.

A new architecture was born in New York. "Your skyscrapers are too small; there are too many of them", said L-C in 1935 (headline in "New York Herald").

1946–47. The UN affair. Minority report by Le Corbusier against the decisions of the commission. The latter wanted to buy 40 square miles – 26,500 acres – in other words, three times the area of Manhattan for Mr. Trygve Lie's typewriters, which flattered and pleased him immensely. In the end the commission got 17 acres, or 1,500 times less! For this site Le Corbusier designed "Model 23 A", which introduced to New York a sample of the "Ville-Radieuse" along the East River, and which will certainly decide the general evolution of the city. By 26th February 1947 L-C had everything ready in New York. Harrisson had told him "Hurry up; the other experts of the commission will be arriving on 15th March". The rest we know. A new skyscraper, which every one calls the "Le Corbusier building", has appeared in New York, the first of its kind. L-C was stripped of all his rights, without conscience and without pity. Every standard of friendship and common decency was flouted (see L-C's prophecy about the future of New York, page 126).

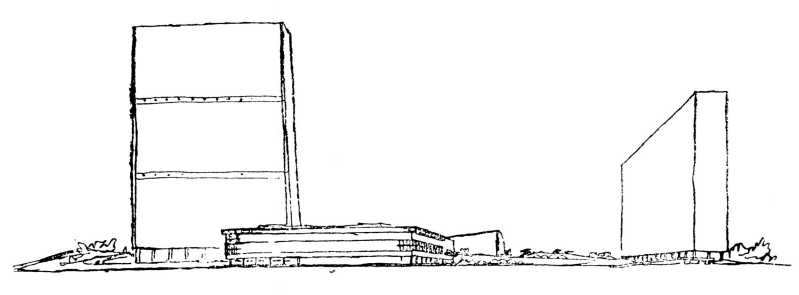

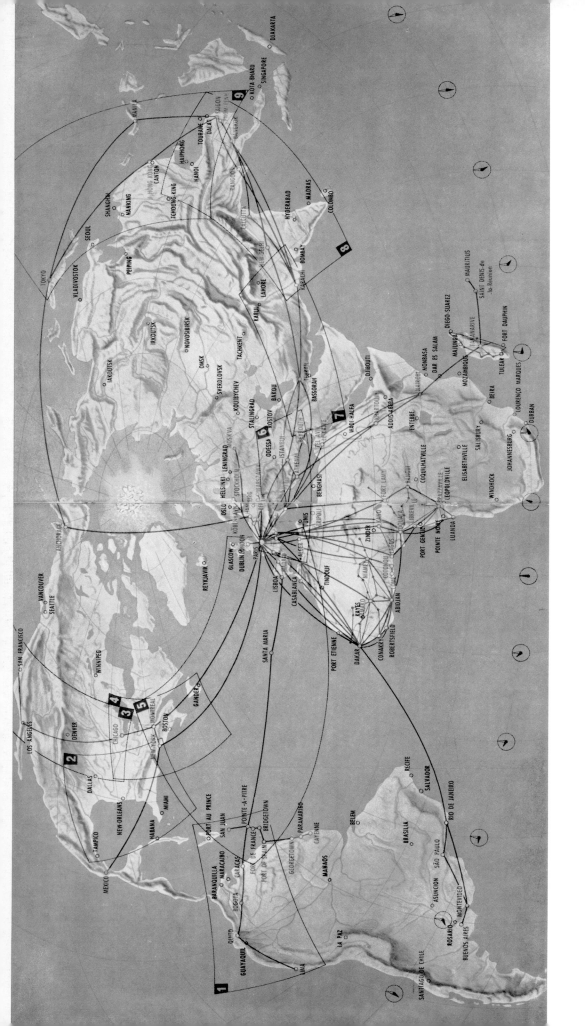

The Planisphere. The world now has 24 solar hours at its disposal.
Marco Polo took his time. Nowadays we say: "Here are your papers, Sir, your contract and your airline ticket. Leaving at six to-night, you will be in the antipodes to-morrow. You will discuss, you will sign and, if you wish, you can start back the same evening and be home next day." We are talking of course of the President of X .... Y .... or Z ...., but we might equally well be referring to a departmental head, a financier, an electrical engineer, an irrigation expert, an agricultural consultant, a geologist, or a surgeon .... From now on men go their ways armed with what they want for discussion. *And the whole world has changed* because of it! Nobody suspected this. Nobody suspected it a century ago when the industrial revolution was beginning. Nations, religions, principalities, powers, going to sleep, waking up, everything is different, changing, moving, flexible. A prodigious new broom has swept through the world order.

The planisphere is no longer developed on both sides of the equator where the liners used to pass, but about the Pole, because one gains twenty hours by going to Tokyo via the Pole rather than by following a parallel!

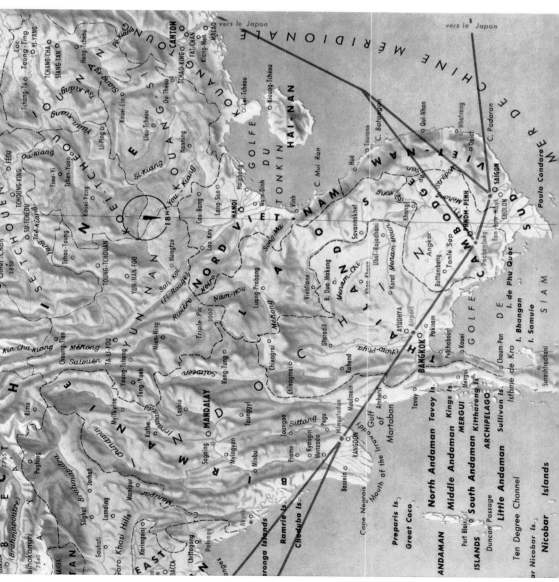

153

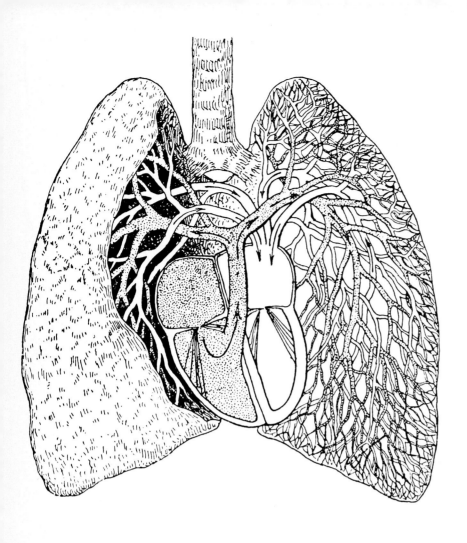

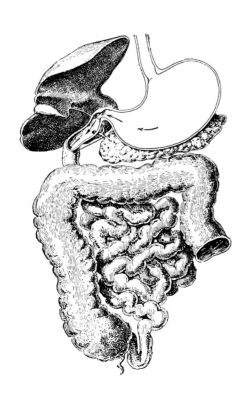

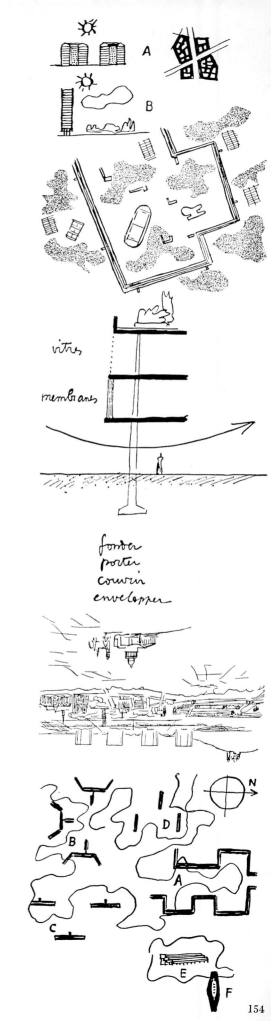

vitres

membranes

fonder
porter
couvrir
envelopper

154

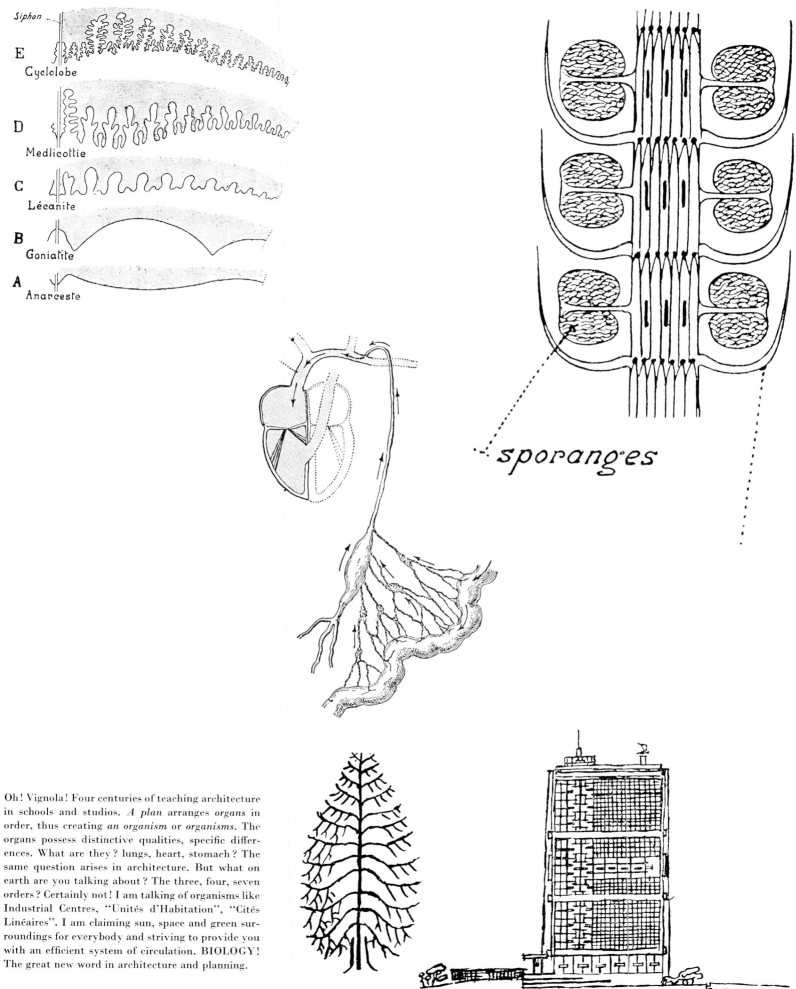

E
Cyclolobe

D
Medlicottie

C
Lécanite

B
Goniatite

A
Anarceste

Siphon

sporanges

Oh! Vignola! Four centuries of teaching architecture in schools and studios. *A plan* arranges *organs* in order, thus creating *an organism* or *organisms*. The organs possess distinctive qualities, specific differences. What are they? lungs, heart, stomach? The same question arises in architecture. But what on earth are you talking about? The three, four, seven orders? Certainly not! I am talking of organisms like Industrial Centres, "Unités d'Habitation", "Cités Linéaires". I am claiming sun, space and green surroundings for everybody and striving to provide you with an efficient system of circulation. BIOLOGY! The great new word in architecture and planning.

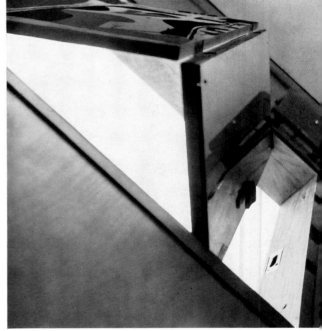

L-C owns a little place by the sea, 12 ft. × 12 ft. and
7 ft. 6 in. high; the whole thing set on a rock 70 ft. above
the water. In this little cabin were devised the venti-
lators which are now a part of the *"undulating glass
panel system":* 1) Sun-control; 2) fresh air to breathe;
3) automatic cross-ventilation by gravity throughout
the day and night; 4) complete protection from mos-
quitoes and other insects.

A site hut, about 6 ft. 6 in. × 13 ft., some dozen yards
from the cabin on a rock, completes the equation:
one for *work*, one for *rest*. The photos show their inse-
parable unity: "architecture and planning" = favourable siting, circulation, views (inside and out),
ventilation (air constantly renewed and even tempe-
rature).

Note: Building a home like this is forbidden by
the bye-laws.

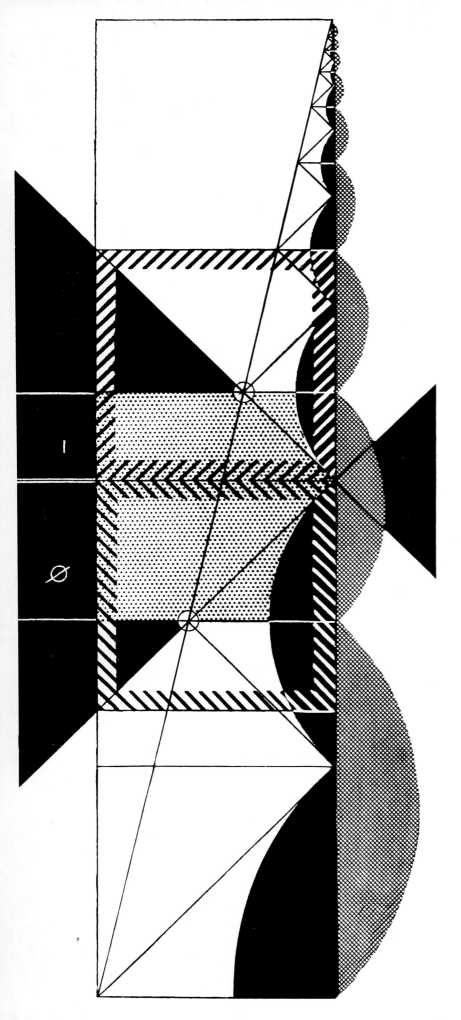

The Modulor opened the way to the future industrial prefabrication of the home. A member of the Economic Council of France, L-C made a contribution (in "La Charte de L'Habitat") on classified sizes *("Nomenclateurs")*. Some day this will form one of the essential factors in the organization of processes in the field of building.

Modulor series as used by L-C (without any frills).

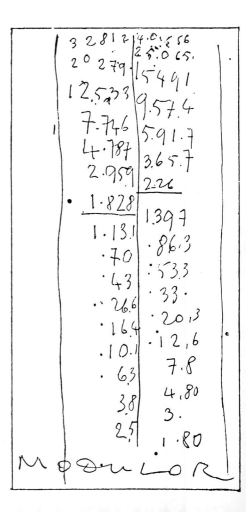

3 2 8 1 2	4.0.56
2 0 2 7 9.	2 5.0 65.
12.533	15491
7.746	9.57.4
4.787	5.91.7
2.959	3.65.7
• 1.828	2.26
1.13.1	1.397
.70	.86.3
.43	.53.3
•.26.6	.33.
•.16.4	.20,3
•.10.1	.12,6
• 6.3	7.8
3.8	4.80
2.5	3.
	1.80

MODULOR

Modulor 1942–1948–1955. Simply and solely a scale of dimensions which enables things to be built for man's use with the help of mathematics. It is a framework enclosing man's movements, whether standing, sitting or lying down. Doctor Andreas Speiser (a mathematician) has written that this was the first occasion that systems of proportion had been based on a man's *height*.

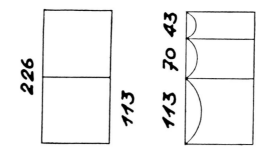

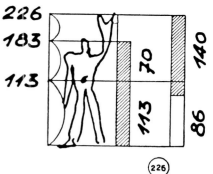

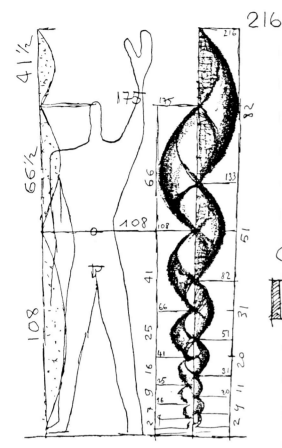

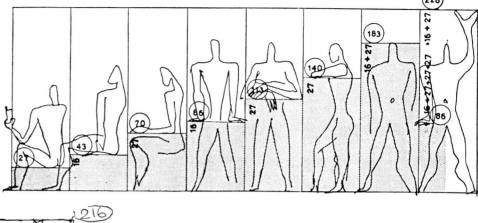

1949. BOOK

LEMODULOR
Editions l'Architecture d'Aujourd'hui
Boulogne s. S.

à bord du Cargo
"Vernon S. Hood"
Le 6 janvier 1946
L-C

The spiral of the Modulor was worked out during the (Atlantic) crossing of the cargo ship "Vernon S. Hood", on 6 January 1946.
This graphic expression of the Modulor was discovered by Justin Serralta and Maisonnier of the atelier at 35 rue de Sèvres (page 158).

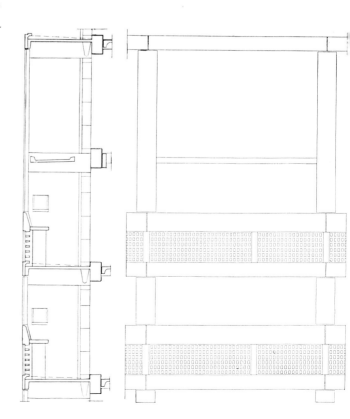

The basic element of the "Unité d'Habitation de Marseille": the "case" to contain a family. This is a significant product of the Modulor.

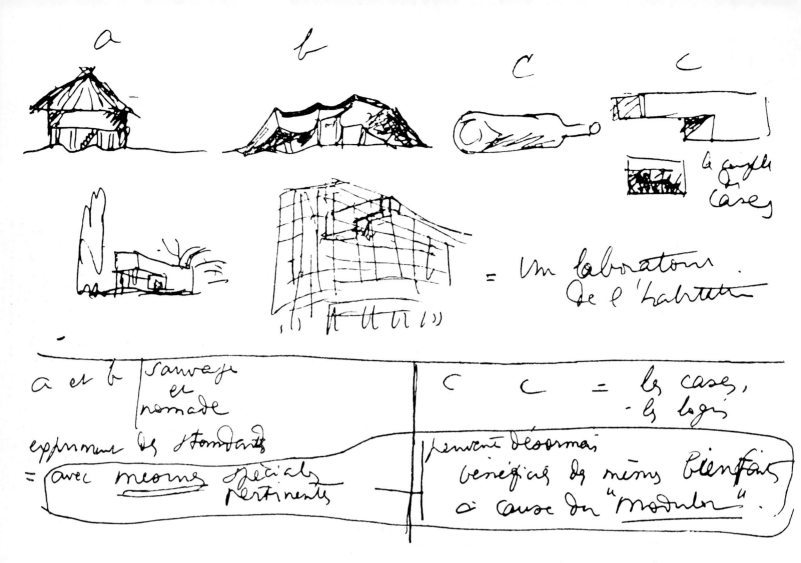

a et b | sauvage et nomade
expriment des Standards
= avec mesures spéciales pertinentes

c c = les cases, - les logis
peuvent désormais bénéficier des mêmes Bienfaits à cause du "Modulor".

= Un laboratoire de l'habitation

1947—1948. CONFERENCES

New York
Bogota
Paris
Milan

One thing suggests another. The Modulor led to reflection on native huts, the nomad's tent, the modern home.

As the structural work of the Unité of Marseilles proceeded, the theory of the "*bin*" and the "*bottle*" began to take shape. The "bottle" is the "dwelling unit"; the "bin" or bottle stand is its means of support. From the nomad and the savage we

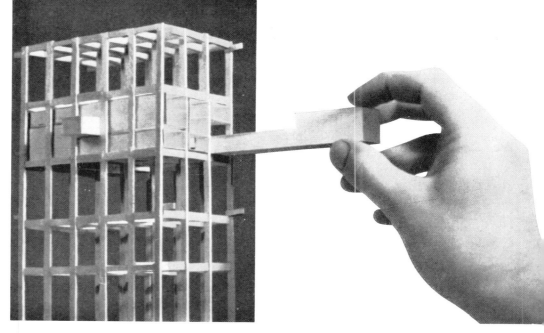

arrive quite logically at the *plan for South Marseilles*. And from now on the door is open to the great metallurgical industry. Things said in 1920 (in L'Esprit Nouveau) about the motor car have become the considered practice of 1960. Forty years of exhaustive and indefatigable study, inside and out. Everything is expressed, displayed, analysed, grouped and formulated in its effects

The "Unité" of the Boulevard Michelet. (The small black rectangular patch represents 360 dwellings with communal services; the extensive white area represents 360 dwellings in the form of individual houses.)

Part of plan for South Marseilles.

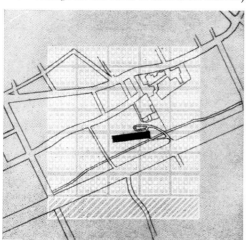

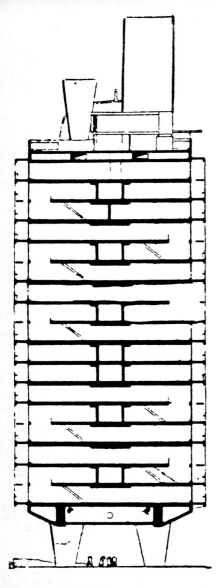

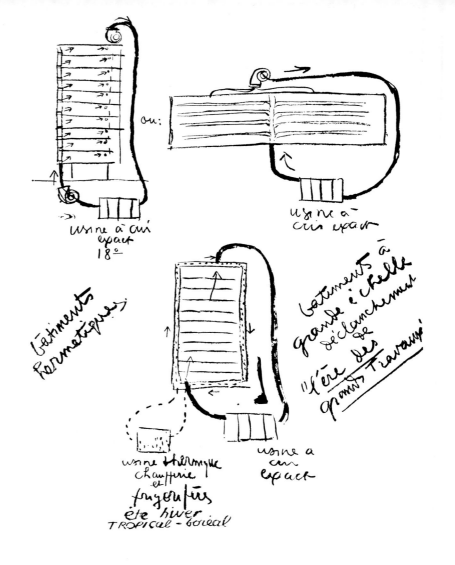

usine à air
epact
18°

ou:

usine à
air epact

bâtiments
hermétiques

bâtiments à
grande échelle
déclenchement de
l'ère des
grands Travaux

usine thermique
chaufferie et
frigorifies
été hiver
TROPICAL - boréal

usine à
air
epact

upon the home: AIR, SOUND, LIGHT, THE "GREEN" TOWN, RECREATION AT ONE'S DOORSTEP. Rediscovering the dignity of walking; dispensing with mass transport, source of so much wasted time to-day; harmonious apportionment of a solar day of 24 hours; invention of "*neutralizing walls*" (1928), etc. ... Electric energy was needed (replacing the paraffin lamp and incandescent burner): thermal electricity, hydraulic electricity, atomic electricity, tide-driven electricity, motor-driven electricity .... The opportunities are limitless; the door is wide open.

The roof, and a landscape worthy of Homer. 800,000 inhabitants of Marseilles do not see the Marseilles landscape. Here, from each of the 700 loggias there is a view of the mountains and the sea. The inhabitants go up to the roof, and the children play there .... When it was all finished, as has been said earlier, a society for the preservation of the French countryside sued L-C for 20 million francs damages for ruining the landscape of France.

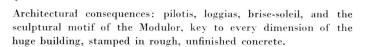

←

Architectural consequences: pilotis, loggias, brise-soleil, and the sculptural motif of the Modulor, key to every dimension of the huge building, stamped in rough, unfinished concrete.

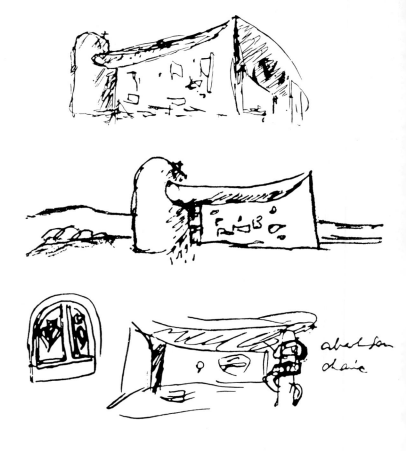

1950–1955. Freedom: Ronchamp. Completely uninhibited architecture. No stipulations except the celebration of the mass, one of the oldest of mankind's institutions. An important influence, however, was there – the countryside, and the horizon on all four sides. These decided the design, and the phenomenon of *"visual acoustics"* appeared. *"Visual acoustics found formal expression"*. Forms make a noise and are silent; some speaking, others listening ....

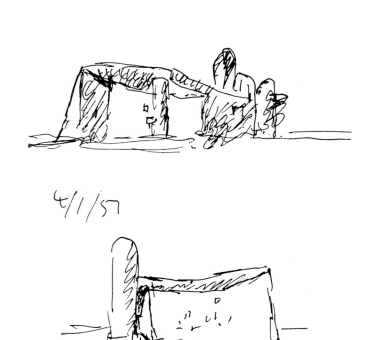

A strange unanimity inspired world opinion, including even
the Church of Rome. A place of mass pilgrimage on fixed
dates, but also a place of pilgrimage for individuals from
the four quarters of the globe, by car, by train, by aeroplane.
They come to Ronchamp.

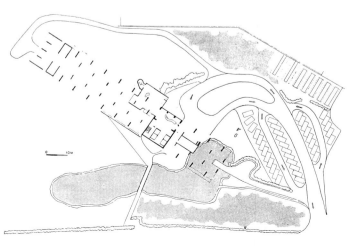

1953–1955, Nantes-Rezé. The press, completely occupied in blocking the road to Marseilles (the "Unité" of the Boulevard Michelet) had failed to notice that we were building the "Unité d'Habitation" of Nantes-Rezé. It was done in eighteen months. These "Housing Units of Proportional Size" are a joy to children (in their rooms, round the family table, in the garden, on the roof). It was left for Berlin to discover, in 1957, that buildings like these are only suitable for bachelors and childless couples (when the "Unité" was being built on the magnificent site offered to L-C on the olympic hill). As a result everything was messed up (see below, page 189).

Dominican Monastery at La Tourette, near Lyon. The site was a steeply sloping valley, wreathed with woods and opening on to a plain. L-C made his design develop from the horizontal of the terrace-roof – a grand, all-commanding, horizontal. Beneath it, are a hundred monks' cells and, below these, are rooms for study and meditation, while lower still are the refectories. At the bottom, partly touching the ground, are the kitchens. The structure is thus linked to the ground by pilotis. The cloister, cruciform, leads to the church, which is in modest rough concrete without mouldings. Thin bands of light are arranged horizontally and vertically, and "canyons of light" stream down upon the monks at their worship from the highest point of the church, or enter from the side to bathe in brilliance the crypts where mass is celebrated in silence.

Tokyo, Cultural Centre and Museum of Western Contemporary Art. The Matsukata collection was handed over to the Japanese government by the French government on condition that a museum would be built to house it. The Japanese government invited Le Corbusier to design the Cultural Centre, of which the Museum is the first section to be built.

Here the Museum occupies the right and lower part of the illustration. The work has been admirably carried out by one-time Japanese draughtsmen at 35 rue de Sèvres, now leading Tokyo architects.

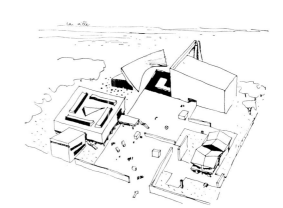

1954. CONFERENCE

Milan

1950. BOOK

POESIE SUR ALGER
Editions Falaise, Paris

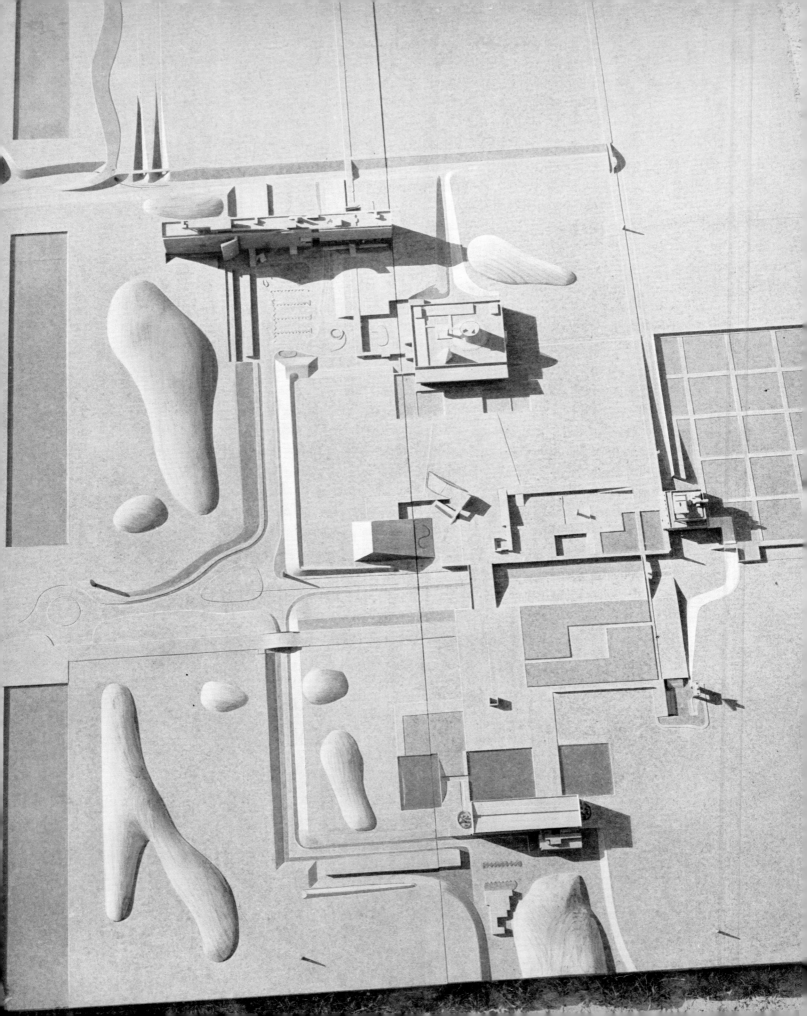

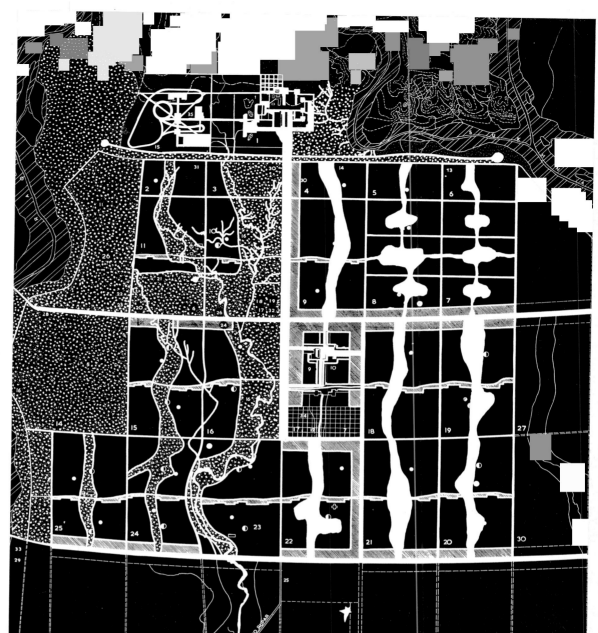

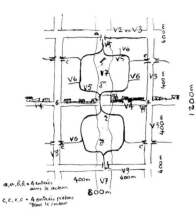

In practice, L-C has not been able to express the principle of the sectors exactly as they were intended.

←

Model of the Capitol, Chandigarh. Buildings already erected: the High Court and the Secretariat. Buildings in course of construction: Parliament, the "Museum of Knowledge".

Chandigarh, capital of the Punjab (India), under construction.

L-C is responsible for the Capitol: the layout, the park, the segregation of cars from pedestrians, the buildings, the monuments with their characteristic symbols representing "the 24 Solar Hours", "the Course of the Sun", "the Tower of Shade", "the Martyr's Monument", the "Open Hand" and, not least, the preservation of the landscape. He is also responsible for the general plan of the city.

The features of this plan are "sectors" (800 × 1200 metres), which are used for the first time. These sectors are enclosed by "V 3s", roads allocated to mechanical transport, to which there is no direct access from the houses. Each sector embraces the daily 24-hour life of a population which can grow from 5,000 to 25,000 inhabitants, and contains essential services.

"The Open Hand" rises 85 feet high within view of the official buildings visible on the horizon.

↑ Parliament

↑ High Court

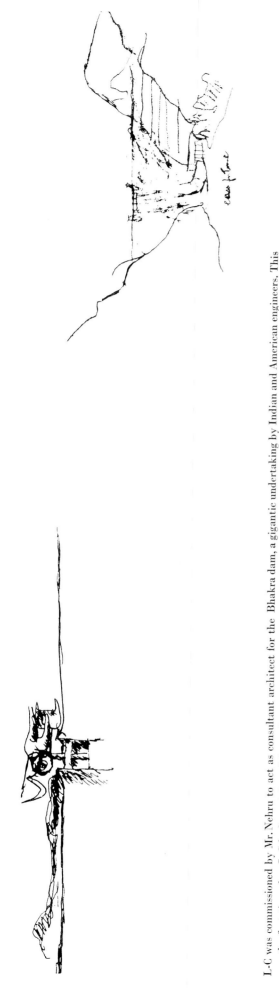

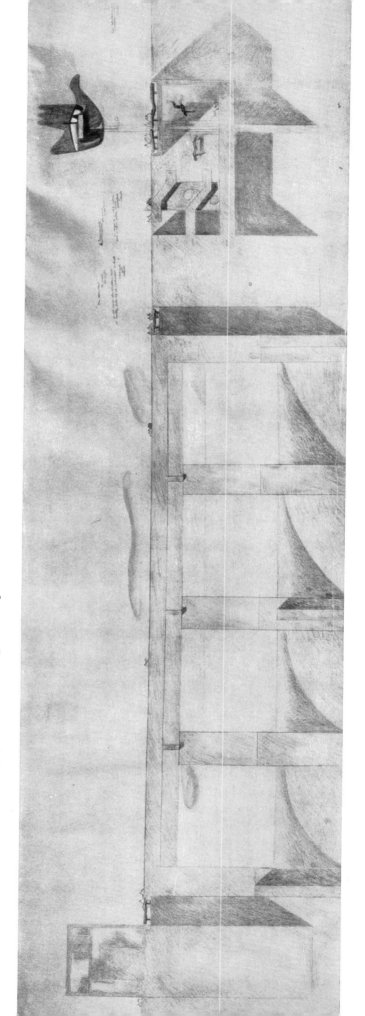

L-C was commissioned by Mr. Nehru to act as consultant architect for the Bhakra dam, a gigantic undertaking by Indian and American engineers. This was the first time that L-C had participated in a scheme of this kind (power house, upper section of dam, organization of approaches and surroundings for tourists). The dam is 200 metres high, and 700 metres long at the top.

Capitol of Chandigarh: Law Courts. Concrete awning protecting the courtrooms from the sun. Brise-soleil in front of the glazed bays of the courts and the high court.

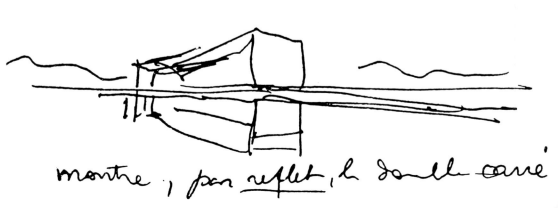

montre, par reflet, le double carré

Secretariat, Ministries' Building: 4,000 employees. Nearly 800 feet long, completely glazed on both fronts and equipped throughout with "undulating glass panels", which are provided with "sun control" (brise-soleil). The building includes two great ramps, each designed for 2,000 employees, climbing like roads to the upper storeys. The lifts are only used for internal services.

Here is the roof.

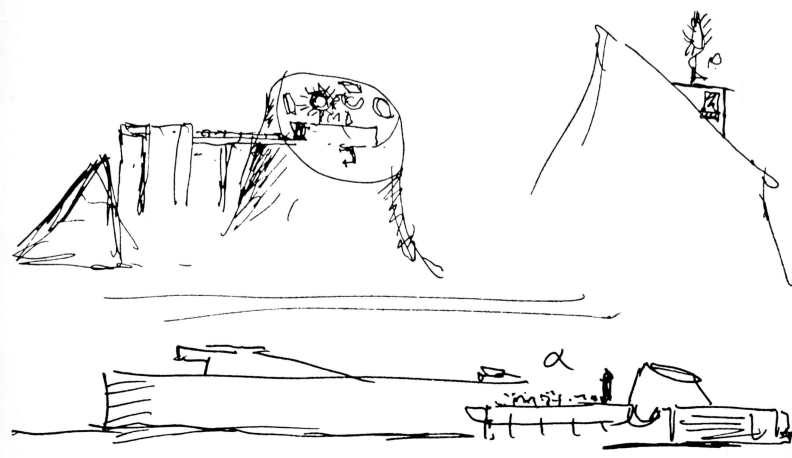

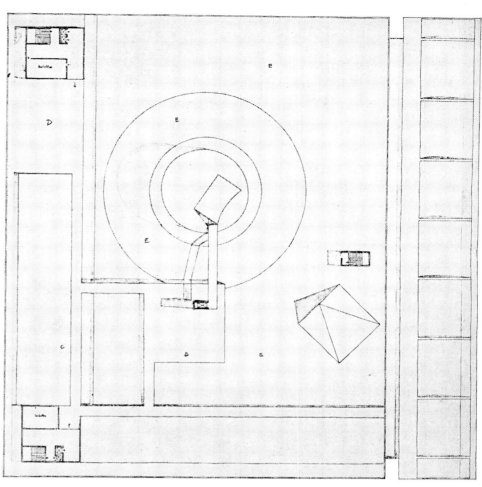

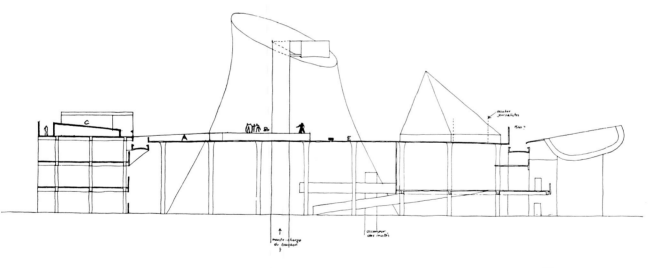

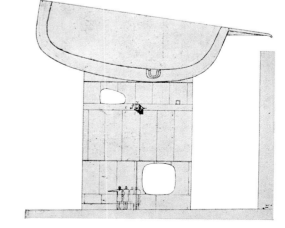

Palace of the (two) Assemblies. Model showing a Lower House (of representatives) and an Upper House (the Senate). Inside, a vast forum and offices; a roof area of over 100,000 sq. ft. forming a garden with a splendid view of the Himalayas. (Under construction in 1960.)

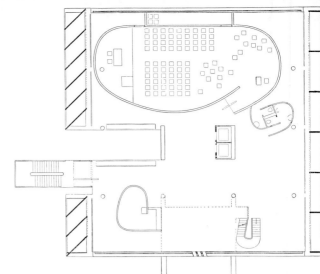

1954 and 1955. BOOKS

UNE PETITE MAISON
(Carnet de la recherche patiente)
Editions Girsberger, Zurich

MODULOR 2
Editions de l'Architecture d'Aujourd'hui,
Boulogne s. S.

←——— ———→

Millowners' Building.

Ahmedabad (centre of the cotton industry
of India), where the climate is very hot.
L-C applied his sun control system to it on
a large scale.

Shodhan House, with its sunshade and hanging gardens.

Ahmedabad Museum. Windowless wall provides insulation. The prominent concrete guttering above the pilotis is intended to accommodate a particular kind of climbing plant which will shade the wall from the sun's heat.

1958. Brussels International Exhibition. Philips Pavilion: Le Corbusier's "Electronic Poem".

L-C had said to Mr. Kalf, one of the directors of Philips: "I shall not give your pavilion a façade, but I shall compose an Electronic Poem contained in a 'bottle'. This bottle will be your pavilion, devoted to the harmonious expression of the unexploited resources of electronics. The Poem will be composed of pictures, coloured rhythms, music. The Electronic Poem will combine in a coherent whole what films, recorded music, colour, words, sound and silence have until now produced independently. The Poem will last ten minutes. It will be performed for 500 spectators at a time. The pavilion will, therefore, be a stomach assimilating 500 listener-spectators, and evacuating them automatically at the end of the performance, in order to provide room for the next five hundred." One million two hundred and fifty thousand visitors experienced the Electronic Poem at the Brussels Exhibition.

The technical preparations lasted two and a half years, including the design and execution of the building, the conception of the Poem, research into its essential features and the final realization in the Philips works at Eindhoven, and also in Amsterdam and Paris. The arrangement of the music was completed superbly by Edgar Varèse in seven months, in a shed specially fitted for the purpose by Philips at Eindhoven. Ten minutes, 600 seconds, (of which 480 were allocated to Edgar Varèse and 120 to Xénakis) entrusted to 400 amplifiers. Philips mobilized their technical services in lighting, sound and film projection, etc., during this exciting preparatory period. In erecting the building, the method of construction was worked out by Professor Vreedenburgh of the University of Delft, while its execution was in the hands of Duyster, engineering-director of the Strabed Company, who built the pavilion with the help of his workpeople and a splendid site-manager, Matthis. Messrs. Kalf and Tak represented the directing staff of Philips in acoustics and lighting; Le Corbusier was responsible for general supervision, assisted by Xénakis, who did the drawings of the pavilion and guided its construction from beginning to end. The film installation was carried out by Agostini of Paris, the mechanical equipment by de Bruyn and Jansen. Electronic, theatrical, and musical, circles had not until then paid much attention to combined enterprises of this sort. Nor was it a trivial matter! Since 35,000 welded connections were needed in the automatic system, by which, when the starting button was finally pressed, everything suddenly sprang into life: light, music, pictures, colours, movement.

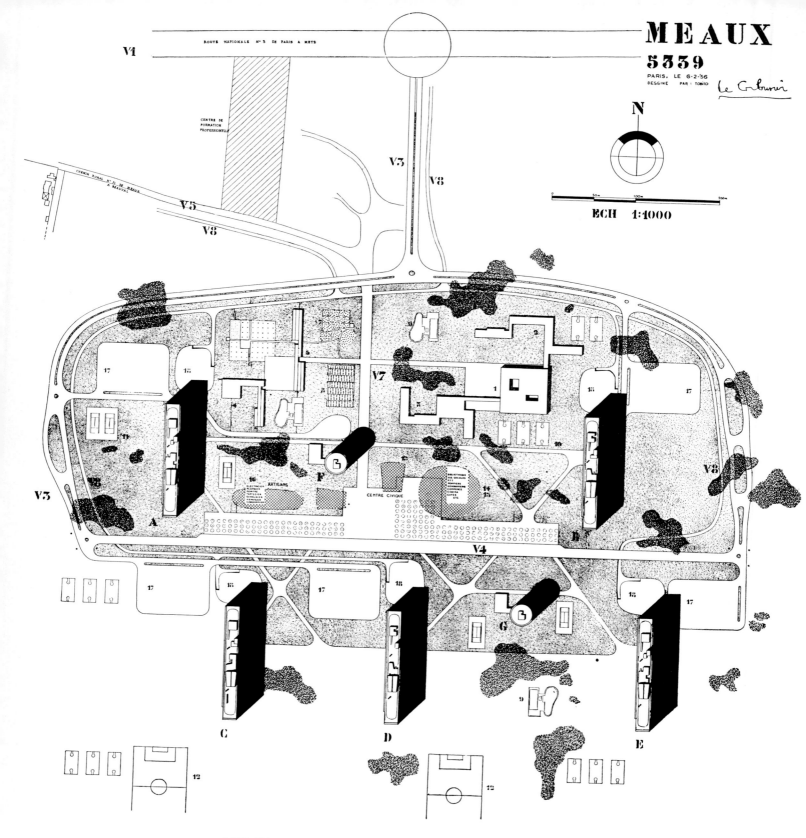

N

ECH 1:1000

1955–1960 ....

Meaux. Erection of five "Housing Units of Proportional Size (Unités d'Habitation ....)". This scheme represents six years of preparatory work. Patience, therefore, is essential. Here will be found separate traffic ways for cars and pedestrians, as well as provision for "individual – collectivity" (schools, clubs, parking places, repair shops for cars and bicycles, swimming pools, "recreation at one's door step", an infants' school on the roof, provision stores in each "Unité" half-way up). Two towers, providing accommodation for single people and a hotel, are important additions to the life of the community. A "V4" serves buildings offering amenities and essential services: the Civic Centre, cinema, library, social insurance, post offices, fire station, police, business offices, cafés, etc. .... The ten thousand inhabitants, thus comfortably established, are directly linked by "V3s" and "V8s" with the "Linear Industrial Centre", which will be set up in the neighbourhood.

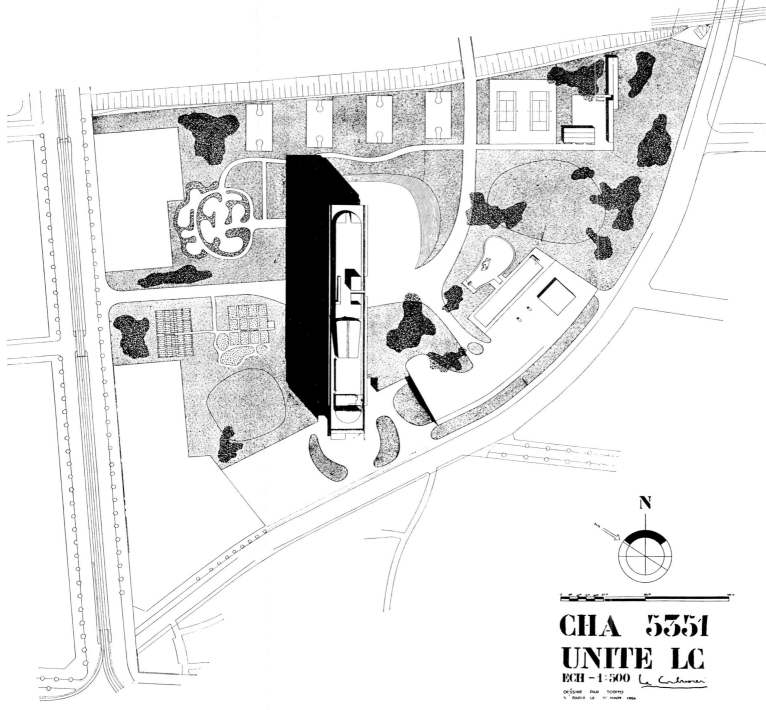

The "Dreieck" site, Berlin. The German government had offered L-C this magnificent setting on the olympic hill of Berlin-Charlottenburg.
This "Unité" was to have been the perfect complement to the one at Marseilles. Actions by the financing company, which could not be prevented, interfered with the execution of the scheme.

1955. CONFERENCE

Berlin

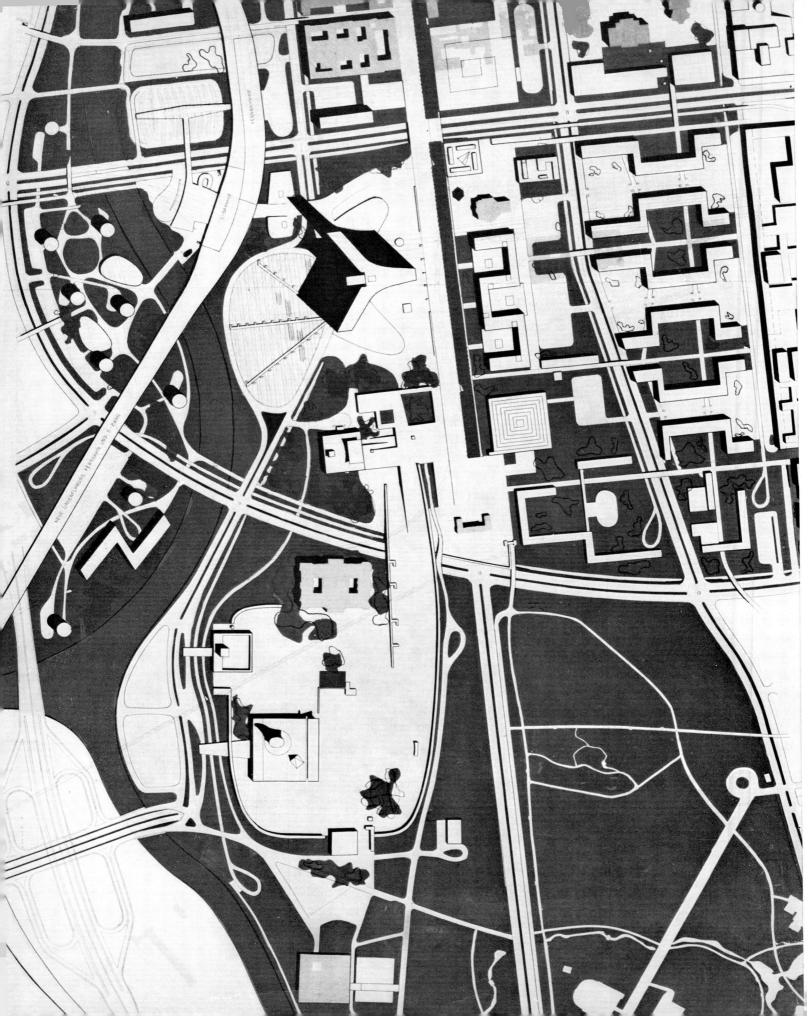

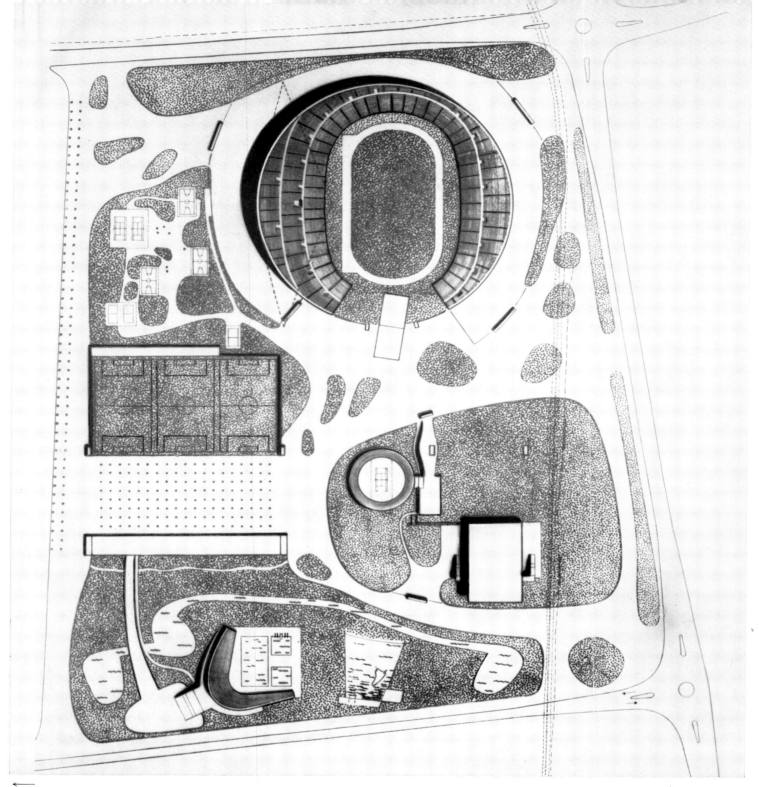

Reconstruction plan for the destroyed centre of Berlin. The most splendid problem that ever confronted L-C, since it entailed replanning a town completely razed to the ground, and rebuilding it as a single conception. L-C accepted the German Government's invitation to take part in the open competition on this occasion, because Walter Gropius had been mentioned as a member of the jury.

151 entries received; 13 selected for consideration. The thirteenth – it was L-C's – was eliminated.

L-C had devoted eight months to its preparation and spent millions of francs ....

Walter Gropius could not go to Germany, as a member of the jury to examine the plans, because he was unwell. 1958. The members of the jury were: Aalto, van Eesteren, Vago, Bartning, Wedepohl etc.

Baghdad. Summoned by the authorities in Irak to build the Baghdad stadium. A stadium to accommodate 55,000; a gymnasium for 6,000 and a swimming pool for 4,000, etc., etc. .... in course of construction.

1956. CONFERENCE

Baghdad

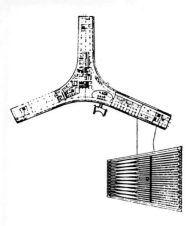

UNESCO Headquarters, Paris. "I feel justified in declaring", said L-C, "that the Committee of 5, comprising, at my suggestion, Walter Gropius, CIAM – Lucio Costa, CIAM – Markelius, CIAM – Rogers, CIAM – and Le Corbusier, CIAM, have established a fundamental and organically effective basis for the Unesco palace, in association with the engineer, Nervi, and with two architects (Breuer and Zehrfuss) nominated at a certain stage by the intervention of the U.S.A. On completing their work, the Committee of 5 handed over to their executives a genuine concrete "organism", adapted to the scale of Paris, occupying the site of the Ecole Militaire, with its very special character, and enjoying a splendid position and delightful views. When the Committee of 5 had completed their deliberations, it was agreed that here was a concrete structure, glazed throughout, suitable for sun-control by brise-soleil". .... But the brise-soleil were not constructed!

Echoes of Zehrfuss come within earshot. "What may appear to some even more astonishing is that the leaders of this new architecture are almost all 'Grands Prix de Rome' winners ...." "To-day it seems that there is a tendency to break away from the somewhat baroque character of Le Corbusier's work and to return to a greater symmetry. This tendency strikes me as logical. While it is a good thing to follow the views of this great theorist, it is probably dangerous to want to put them into an architecture marked so strongly by personality and, if I may say so, with such individuality." (Article published in an important foreign paper, signed by the author referred to above and giving his title of "Premier Grand Prix de Rome", 20 pages of which were entirely devoted to France itself, among them one full page on architecture.

..., ce qui peut sembler à certains encore plus étonnant, les chefs de file de cette architecture nouvelle sont presque tous « Grands Prix de Rome ».

il semble qu'aujourd'hui on ait tendance à s'écarter du caractère quelque peu baroque des œuvre de Le Corbusier pour revenir à des réalisations plus équilibrées. En cela, cette tendance me paraît raisonnable : s'il est bon de suivre ce grand théoricien dans ses vues, il est sans doute dangereux de vouloir

imiter une architecture marquée d'une si forte personnalité et, pourrais-je le déclarer, si individuelle.

Par Bernard-H. ZEHRFUSS
Architecte en chef des Bâtiments civils et Palais nationaux - Grand Prix de Rome

My answer:

"Le Poème de l'Angle Droit"
published by Editions Verve, Paris.
185 large pages with coloured
lithographs. The illustrations
show a reproduction of the last two pages.

On a
avec un charbon
tracé l'angle droit
le signe
Il est la réponse et le guide
le fait
une réponse
un choix
Il est simple et nu
mais saisissable
Les savants discuteront
de la relativité de sa rigueur
Mais la conscience
en a fait un signe
Il est la réponse et le guide
le fait
ma réponse
mon choix.

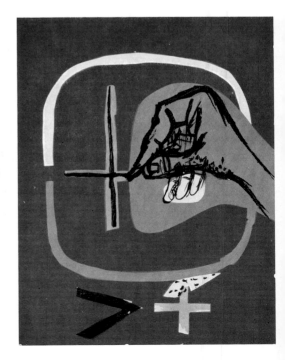

2

Part 2

A PROFESSION

je pense que si l'on accorde quelque signification à mon œuvre d'architecte, c'est à ce labeur secret qu'il faut en attribuer la valeur profonde

L-C 1948

ACROBAT

An acrobat is no puppet.

He devotes his life to activities
in which, in perpetual *danger of death*,
he performs extraordinary movements
of infinite difficulty, with disciplined
exactitude and precision .... free
to break his neck and his bones and
be crushed.

Nobody asked him to do this.
Nobody owes him any thanks.
He lives in an extraordinary world, of the acrobat.
Result: most certainly! He does things
which others cannot.
Result: why does he do them?
others ask. He is showing off;
he's a freak; he scares us; we pity him;
he's a bore.

1 The studio of patient research

"In gratitude to my wife for thirty five years of wonderful devotion,
for surrounding me
with the blessings of quiet, affection and happiness ...."

(L-C)

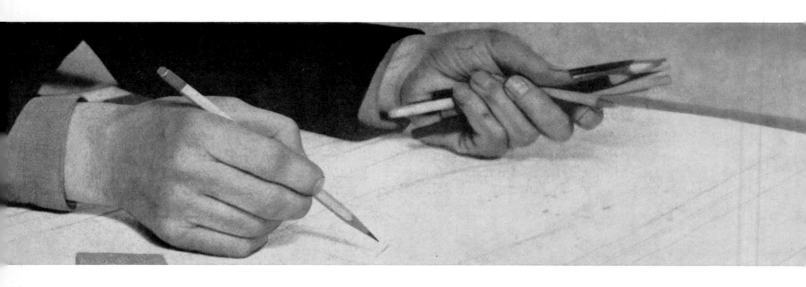

DRAWING

We learn to see how things are born. We see them develop, grow, change, blossom, flourish and die .... And the grain matures.

The fundamental principle is "from the inside out" (contrary to appearances). Everything in life is in essence biological. The biology of a plan or section is as necessary and obvious as that of a creature of nature. The introduction of the word *"biology"* illuminates all researches in the field of building. Living, working, cultivating body and mind, moving from place to place, are parallel processes to those of the blood, nervous and respiratory systems.

From the inside out .... The value of all things lies in their purpose, in the germinating seed. Nothing is seen, admired or loved except what is so fine and beautiful that from the outside one penetrates into the very heart of the thing by study, research and exploration.

By devious ways, we therefore reach the centre.

5 March 1960.

2 Drawing (observing - discovering - inventing - creating)

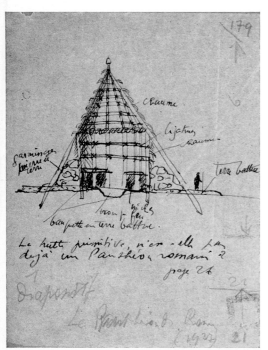

La hutte primitive, n'est-elle pas
déjà un Panthéon romain ?
page 26

Le Panthéon de Rome

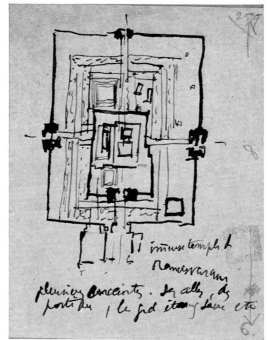

immense temple de
Rameswaram.

plusieurs enceintes. des allées, des
portiques, le fond étant sacré etc.

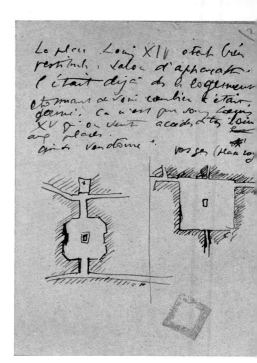

La place Louis XIV était très
vestibule, salon d'apparat.
C'était déjà du logement
les mauvais de voir combien c'était
dessiné. Ce n'est que sous Louis
XV qu'on veut accéder très bien
aux places.
après Vendôme.

Vosges (place royale)

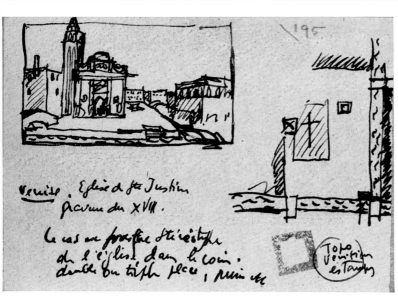

Venise. Église de Ste Justine
gravure du XVIII.

Le cas ne paraît si véritable
de l'église, dans le coin.
double ou triple place, plein air

Photo
Vénitien
estampes

S. Giorgio dei Greci

Aspect construit des contrastes verticaux à volume
le haut du campanile se condense

Photo
Véni...

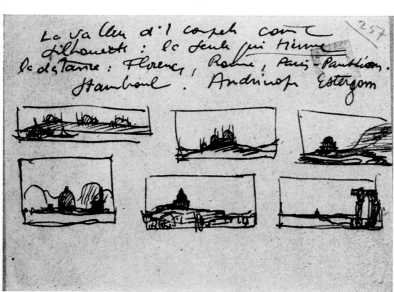

La valeur d'1 corps en
silhouette : le seul qui tienne
le drame : Florence, Rome, Paris=Panthéon.
Stamboul. Andrinople Estergom

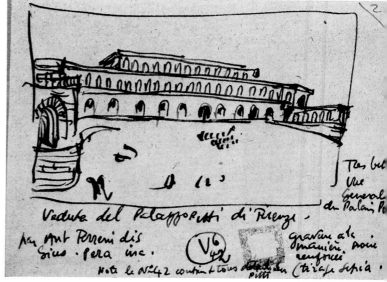

Veduta del Palazzo Pitti di Firenze.

par Ant. Terreni dis
Sius. Pera inc.

V 6
42

Note le N° 42 contient tous détails en
Pitti

Très belle
vue
générale
du Palais Pitti

gravure à la
manière noire
renforcée
(tirage sépia)

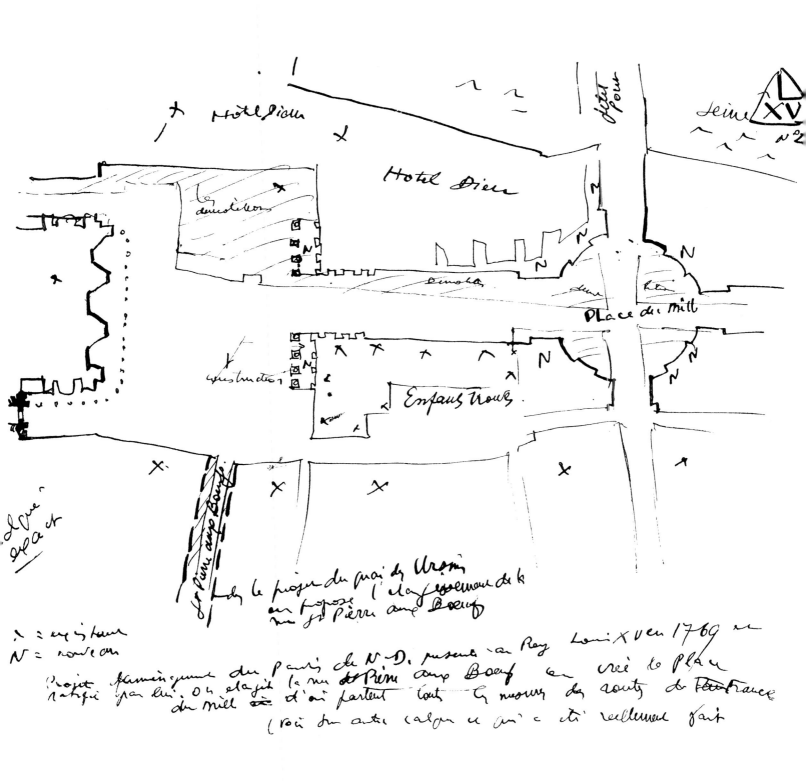

1915. Research in the Bibliothèque Nationale, Paris (Prints Department). By working with our hands, by drawing, we enter the house of a stranger and are enriched by the experience. We learn.

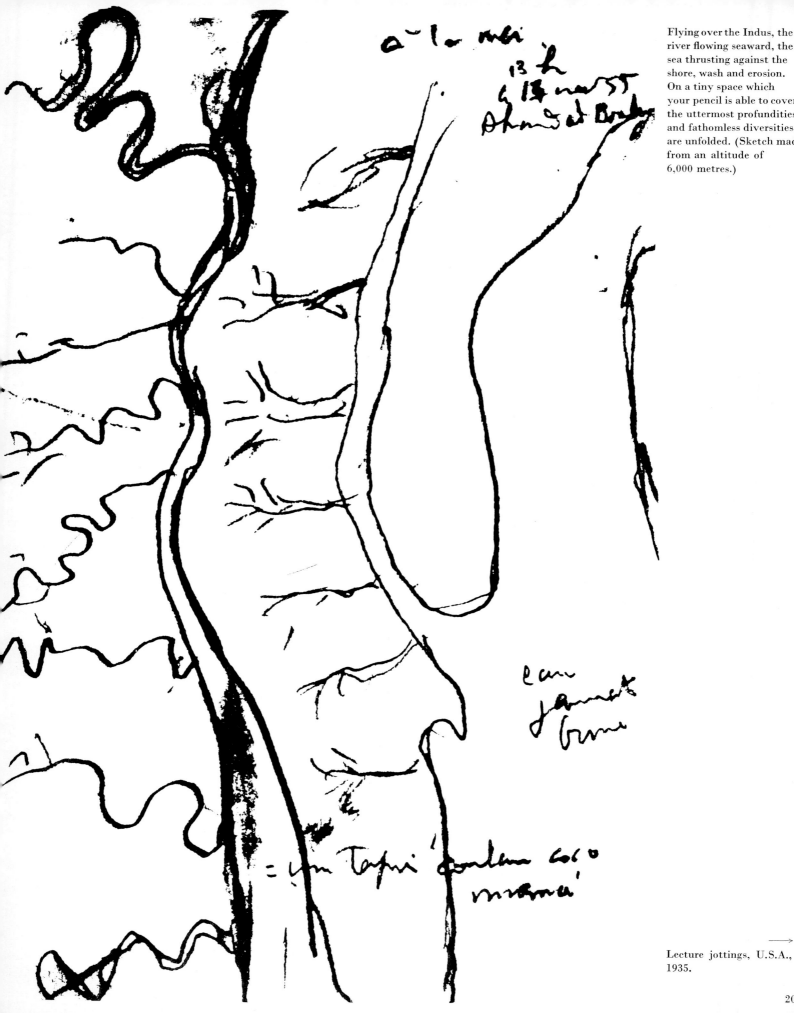

Flying over the Indus, the river flowing seaward, the sea thrusting against the shore, wash and erosion. On a tiny space which your pencil is able to cover, the uttermost profundities and fathomless diversities are unfolded. (Sketch made from an altitude of 6,000 metres.)

Lecture jottings, U.S.A., 1935.

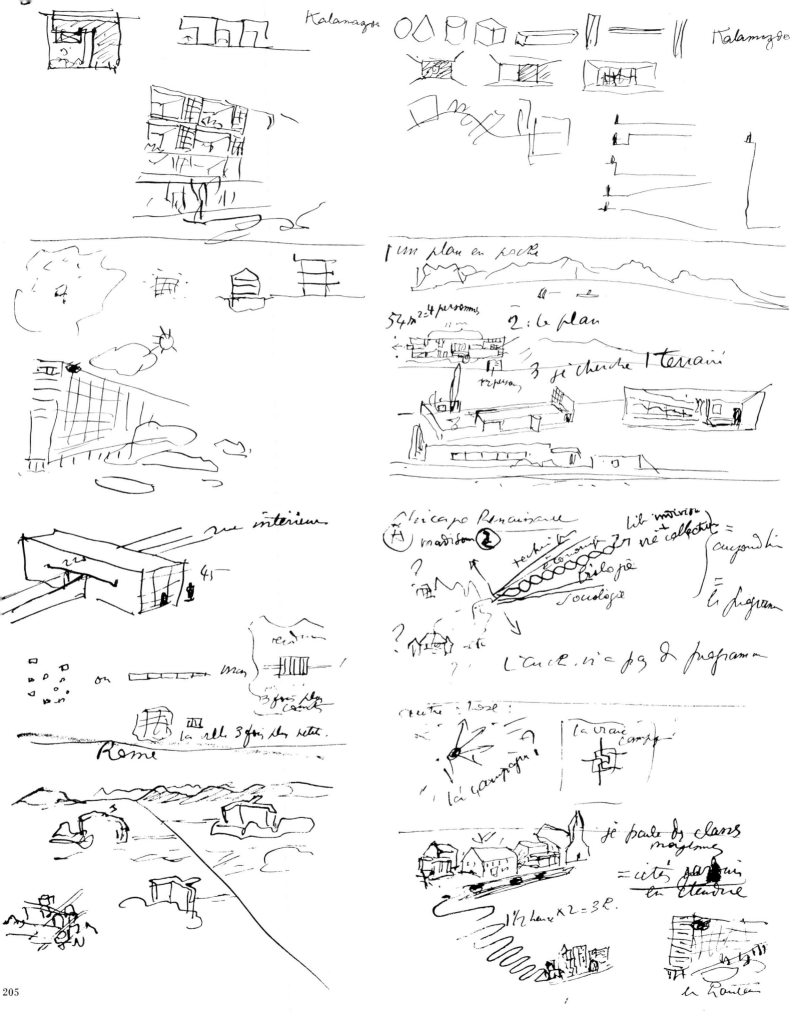

Kalamazoo

Kalamazoo

un plan en poche

54 m² = 4 personnes

2: le plan

3 je cherche 1 terrain

repusam

rue intérieur

Chicago Renaissance
madison

aujourd'hui

le diagramme

L'arch. n'a pg de programme

rendu

3 fois plus court

la cellule 3 fois plus petite.

Rome

la vraie campagne

la campagne

je parle des clans
= cités
en étendre

1½ heure × 2 = 3 R.

Kalamazoo

1927. The Sketchbook.

1919

1925

207

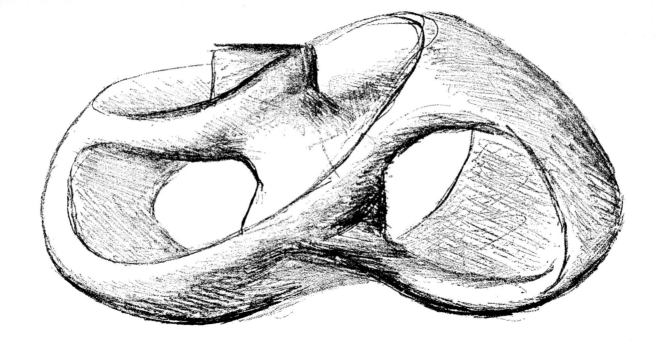

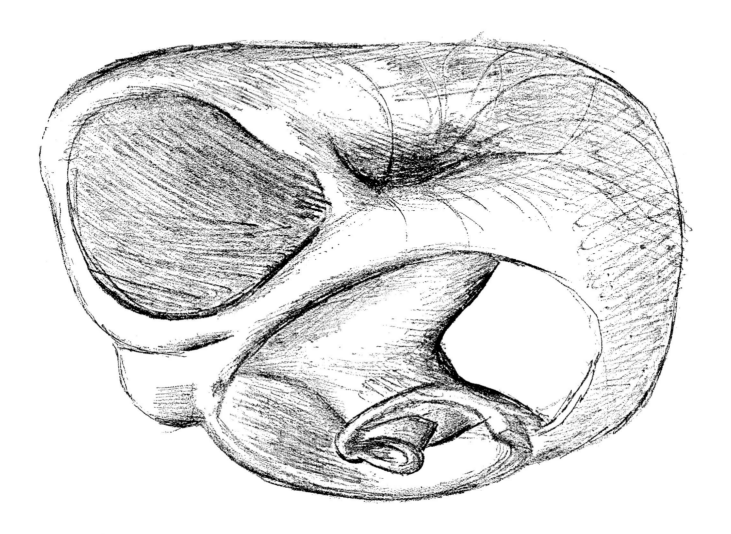

Everywhere objects like these are spread before
us. If you have a pencil in your hand, look at them
and you will understand; you will then have a
storehouse of inspiration to draw upon, the lessons taught by natural phenomena. The chance
occurrence, too: the broken shell, the shoulder of
beef sliced by the butcher's saw, have riches to
offer which the mind cannot conceive.

209

Some truths projected
from the drawing office of
Chandigarh. "Gentlemen,
they all have a head and
a tail, two arms and two
legs. Enough to make a
rule and to show that
variety has no limits."

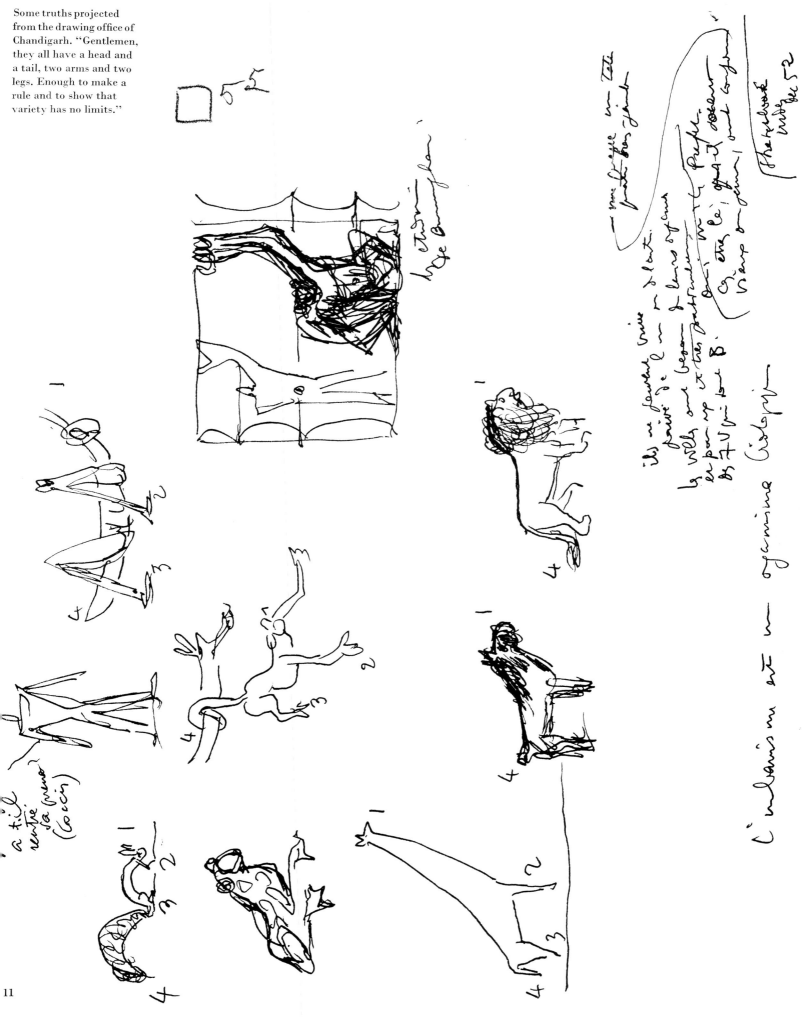

11

Graffiti at Cap-Martin (fragment), about 13×8 ft., 1938.

12 avril
52 (2)

Government Building, Chandigarh, in its natural setting.
Now replaced by the Palais du Gouvernement and Musée
de la Connaissance.

The Sainte-Baume episode. It is written in man's destiny that he abominates constructive
ideas. Among myriads of struggling people, myriads of miles, and myriads of fleeting hours,
something is occasionally attained by luck and, as the centuries pass, time rewards the
achievement. But those who strive to unite the things of men with the things of nature in
immediately effective harmony find themselves bitterly repulsed and gain nothing. It is
against the rules. So the surface of the water is once more undisturbed; all is well; every one
can sleep peacefully! And yet ....

en A l'hôtel alvéolaire de 24 m d'épaisseur

"Des Capitales", an exhibition by L-C, principally organised by Boesiger which toured the whole of Europe, one part of America, and one part of Asia 1957–1960 . . . .

3 No beginning and no end
   a. Painting
   b. Sculpture
   c. Architecture and Town and Country planning - their
      supreme and interdependent rôle

"Icone 1" (BULLS series), 1955. 64 × 51 in.

Date 6. 1. 60. Flying over the Nile Delta. (New Delhi—Paris aircraft)

"Painting is a bitter struggle, terrifying, pitiless, unseen; a duel between the artist and himself. The struggle goes on inside, hidden on the surface. If the artist tells, he is betraying himself! ...."

(L-C's sketchbook)

a. Painting

"The Chimney-piece", 1918. 23 × 19 in. L-C's first picture
(he was 31).

EXHIBITION

"Des Capitales", an exhibition by L-C
1957–58–59–60. In the museums and art institutes
of Zurich, Berlin, Munich, Frankfurt,
The Hague, Stockholm, Copenhagen, London, Rome,
Milan (the same for pictures on pages
221, 223, 224, 225, 232).

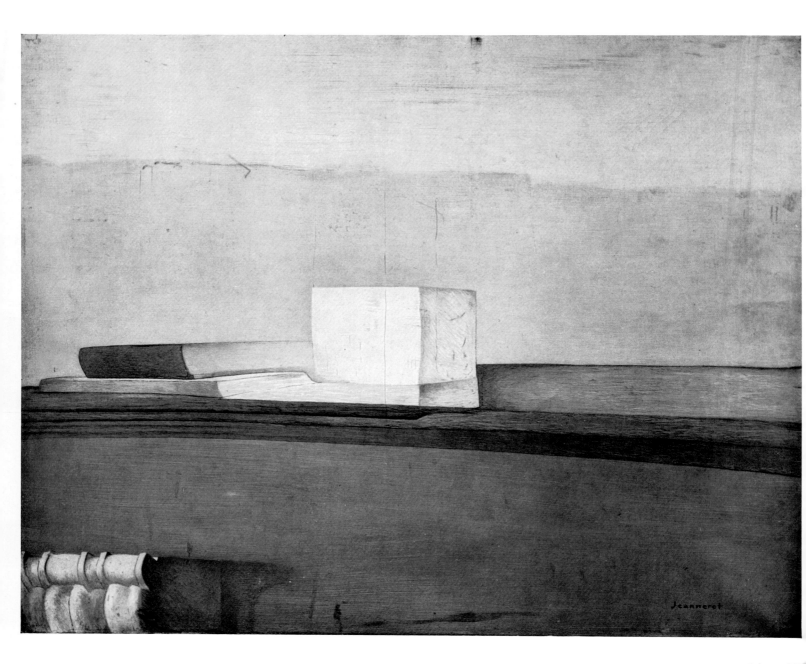

"Still Life with Egg", 1919. 39 × 32 in.

EXHIBITION

Travelling Exhibition of the Institute of Contemporary Art, Boston.
1948–49–50–51–52–53–54–55–56 in the Museums or Institutes of Contemporary Art, Boston, Institute of Arts, Detroit, Museum of Art, San Francisco, Fine Arts Center, Colorado Springs, Museum of Art, Cleveland, City Art Museum of St. Louis. Brasil: Museum of Art, Sao Paulo. Europe: Berlin, Belgrade, Munich, Recklinghausen, Innsbruck, Vienna.

"Violin with Red Case", 1920. 32 × 39 in. La Roche Collection, Paris.

"Upright Guitar", 1920. 39 × 32 in.

"Large Still Life". Salon des Indépendants 1922. 45 × 58 in. Albert Jeanneret Collection.

1923. "Still Life with many things". Salon des Indépendants 1923. 45 × 58 in. Le Corbusier Permanent Collection, Musée d'Art Moderne, Paris.

"Still Life", 1925. 39 × 32 in. Miller Collection, Meridan, U.S.A.

"Still Life", 1926. 39 × 32 in.

Still Life, "Cathedrals of Sens", 1940. 51 × 38 in.

"An Ubu", 1940–1944. 39 × 32 in.

Mural (500 sq. ft.) in the library of the Swiss Pavilion, Cité Universitaire. 1948.

Birth of the "BULLS" series. Sketch made in an aircraft above the Indies from a photo of a picture "Still Life" of 1922 and 1940.

1927–1940. 38 × 55 in.

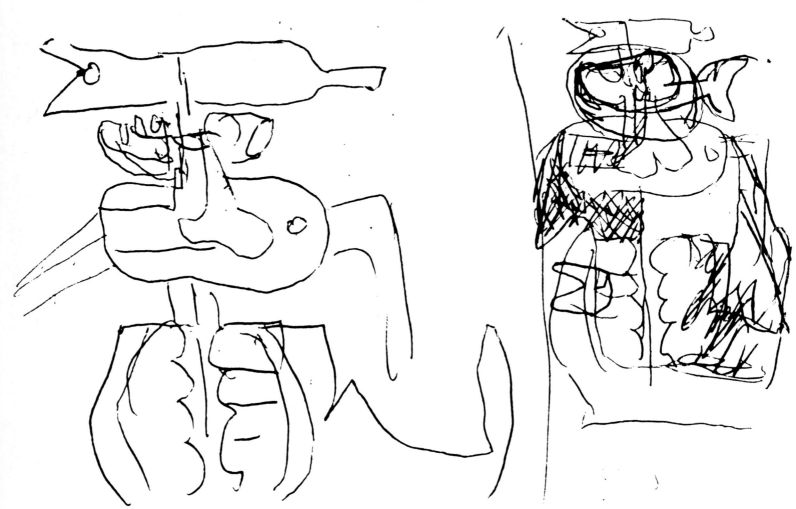

"Bull IV", 1953. 64 × 51 in. At the Bank of Osaka, Japan.

Mural, in an office of the Duval factory at St. Dié; made from a fragment of the 1923 picture (see page 225).

Aubusson tapestry, Marie Cuttoli series. 1936.

EXHIBITIONS

Exhibitions of paintings and sculpture by L-C. Since the first exhibition of 1918 with Thomas of Paris (Exhibition Ozenfant and Jeanneret) and those which followed at the Gallery Druet, Paris 1921, at "L'Effort Moderne" Léonce Rosenberg, Paris 1923, certain essential pieces of the pictorial work of L-C were shown in special exhibitions by various museums, institutes or galleries. Tapestries often accompanied the paintings and sculptures: 1945 New York, Radio City. 1947 Amsterdam, Stedelijk Museum. 1952 Galerie Denise René, Paris. 1938 Galerie Louis Carré, Paris. 1938 Kunsthaus Zurich. 1933 New York, John Becker Gallery. 1953 Musée d'Art Moderne, Paris. 1953 Institute of Contemporary Art, London. 1953 Stockholm, Galerie Samlaren. 1954 Villa del Olmo, Como. 1954 Kunsthalle Berne. 1956 Festival Lyon-Charbonnières. 1957 Tapisseries, Musée de la Chaux-de-Fonds. 1956 Exhibition BULLS, Pierre Matisse Gallery, New York. 1950 and 1952 Exhibition L-C Galerie Paul Rosenberg, New York. All these exhibitions are exclusively devoted to L-C.

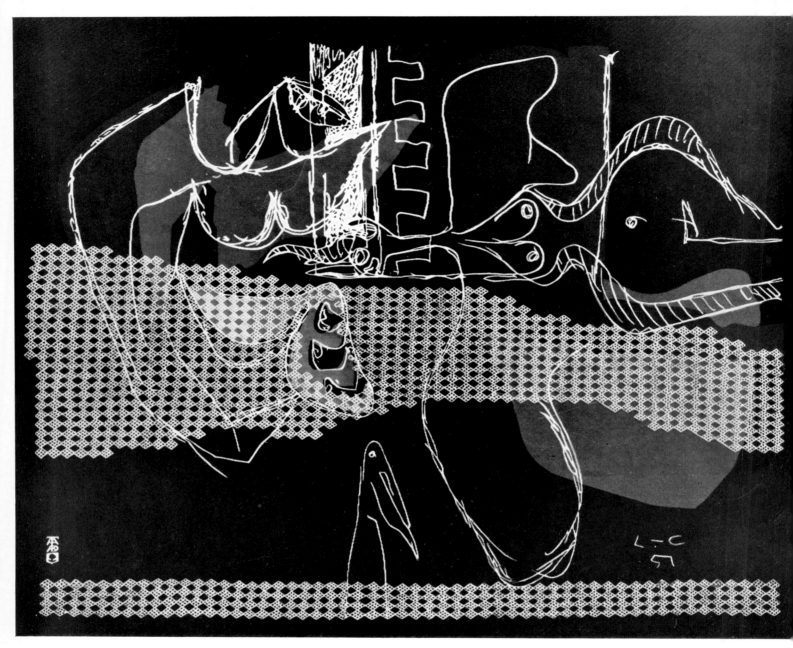

Tapestry "Présences". 5 ft. 9 in. × 7 ft. 3 in. 1951.

Villa del Olmo, Como. 1954.

Aubusson tapestry, "Gentillesses". 7 ft. 3 in. × 9 ft. 1954. Mura
nomad series, executed at Aubusson and Felletin under technic
direction of Pierre Baudouin.

Exhibition L-C: Festival Lyon-Charbonnières. 1956.

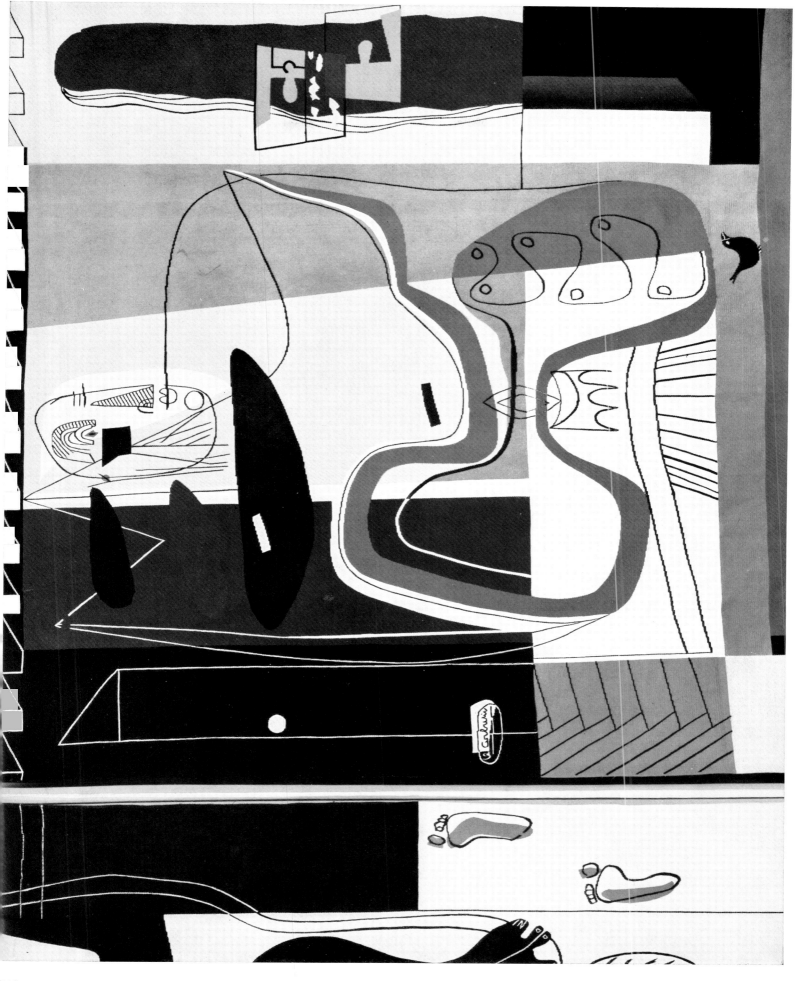

239

Tapestry, approximately 2,000 sq. ft. (curtain for the new theatre, Tokyo, architect Sakakura).

High Court building, Chandigarh: acoustic tapestry for the High Court (Chief Justice's room), approximately 1,500 sq. ft. 1954.

$\longrightarrow$

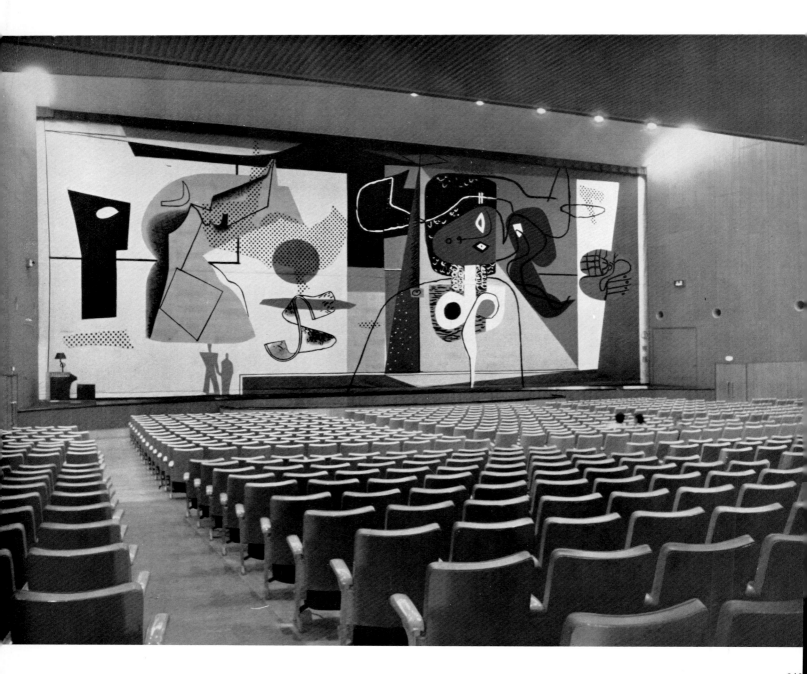

Enamelled door of Ronchamp
Chapel (executed by L-C),
twice 80 sq. ft. = 160 sq. ft.

L ·C
29
44

DU TREFONDS ....

Some of the pictures painted in Paris from 1940 onwards were potential sculpture, many of them with the title "Ubu" (the international scene was full of Ubus ....).

Five years later, Joseph Savina, back from a prison camp in Germany, a Breton wood worker and sculptor and friend of L-C, said to him: "Would you let me use your pictures as models for sculpture?" "What!!" To express light and space comes naturally to L-C; it is part of his character, a fundamental peculiarity. Having worn spectacles since the age of thirteen, he has developed the habit of getting very close to any object which he is drawing, to see "how it's made". To him, it is the outline of things which explains their volume. L-C's pictures represent objects seen from in front, but their depth is implied in the lines. In architecture this trait is very significant, for it is the plan and section uncompromising and precise, which provide the entire basis for his architectural inventions. On reflection, Savina's question was not so startling. There could only be one answer in practice. Savina, wedded to his bench, is no mere amateur. He gets right inside a problem, and really wants to see designs painted or drawn in Paris (sketches, plans and sections) assume in Brittany three-dimensional shape in wood, with finishing touches added in Paris by Savina and L-C together, and coloured by one or the other, or by both. This work goes back to 1945, fifteen years. From time to time large exhibitions of these carvings have been sent on tour. To the field of contemporary plastic art they have contributed a number of new ideas about equipoised sculpture. Some of their parts are movable. They can be dismantled in certain instances and be spread out as several pieces in a room ....

b. Sculpture

In 1930, the first plans for Algiers. In 1945,
the second of L-C's and Savina's sculptures.

In 1935, L-C's first mural painting at
Vézelay and, in 1953, an uncoloured
sculpture.

Walter Gropius collection.

L-C and Savina: Kinetic sculpture in wood, 1950.

Vigorous polychromatic treatment and handling of masses; pathos expressed in equipoise.

Sculpture designed to the Modulor (1953); its parts can be assembled or moved at will.

1942. For the "Heights of Algiers".

A decisive declaration.

As we come to the end of this book, we can draw back and watch things taking shape against the backcloth of the sky. There is no beginning and no end, and only one answer – architecture and planning.

Here is the declaration on the first page of the "Ville Radieuse" in 1934. If this statement is clear and categorical, nevertheless it can still be said that planning to-day languishes in complete obscurity; there is nobody capable of serving its interests. We are speaking here of planning as "evidence of the activity of a civilization" or as "evidence of the activity of a society". And this is a machine civilization and a machine society.

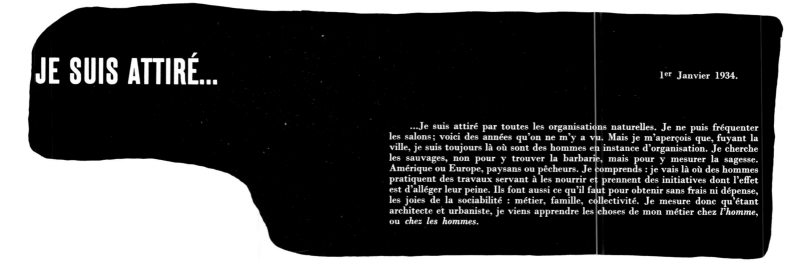

JE SUIS ATTIRÉ...

1er Janvier 1934.

...Je suis attiré par toutes les organisations naturelles. Je ne puis fréquenter les salons; voici des années qu'on ne m'y a vu. Mais je m'aperçois que, fuyant la ville, je suis toujours là où sont des hommes en instance d'organisation. Je cherche les sauvages, non pour y trouver la barbarie, mais pour y mesurer la sagesse. Amérique ou Europe, paysans ou pêcheurs. Je comprends : je vais là où des hommes pratiquent des travaux servant à les nourrir et prennent des initiatives dont l'effet est d'alléger leur peine. Ils font aussi ce qu'il faut pour obtenir sans frais ni dépense, les joies de la sociabilité : métier, famille, collectivité. Je mesure donc qu'étant architecte et urbaniste, je viens apprendre les choses de mon métier chez *l'homme*, ou *chez les hommes*.

c. Architecture and Town and Country planning –
their supreme and interdependent rôle

1926. Cook.

1927. Garches.

Henri Matisse was having tea one day in Stein's house soon after the latter had moved in, when L-C said to him: "What do you think of it?" Matisse,

confused and entirely delighted, replied : "I am utterly at a loss!" That was in 1927.

1929. Villa Savoye.

Monastery of La Tourette.

A concrete door....

.... precise profile of Ronchamp.

No stained glass windows!

Ronchamp.

(See pages 171, 255, 272, 303.) 1,400 inhabitants (pedestrians) enter the house by this single 6 ft. bridge. I announced this fact to the authorities. 1,400 inhabitants in family houses, would necessitate 3 kilometres of roads, communications, water, gas, electricity, telephones. Here the bridge is over the water. Impossible to cheat. It is 50 metres long! That's all! To say such things sounds like a joke, but as for executing them, even to write about them would make one furious. For 4 years the 1,400 inhabitants of Nantes-Rezé passed over the 6 ft. bridge – and never noticed it. (This house was commissioned and paid for by a Co-operative Society.)

Large wooden model of Chandigarh.

The town was supposed to have no water. But it is underground, 250 feet deep and completely pure. A dam has been constructed by extending the Capitol Boulevard, and a splendid lake has been formed. And, taking a homeric stand, L-C has forbidden the lake to motorboats and the top of the dam to bicycles, cars and buses. He has also forbidden any lighting in the evening except "camp-fire" lamps, which make it possible to see the stars in the sky and the stars in the water, the mountains, too, in the water – and all of these things in absolute silence.

A commemoration stone has been presented in gratitude to those who created this lake. It carries, in four languages – Hindi, Punjabi, Urdu and English, the following words:

> "THE FOUNDERS OF CHANDIGARH HAVE OFFERED THIS LAKE
> AND DAM TO THE CITIZENS OF THE NEW CITY SO THAT THEY
> MAY ESCAPE THE HUMDRUM OF CITY LIFE AND ENJOY THE
> BEAUTY OF NATURE IN PEACE AND SILENCE."

At the height of the dispute over the absence of water, L-C named this boulevard, which forms a frontage for the town and faces the Himalayas, the "Boulevard of the Waters" and made two lakes 2 1/2 miles long.

Ministries Building.

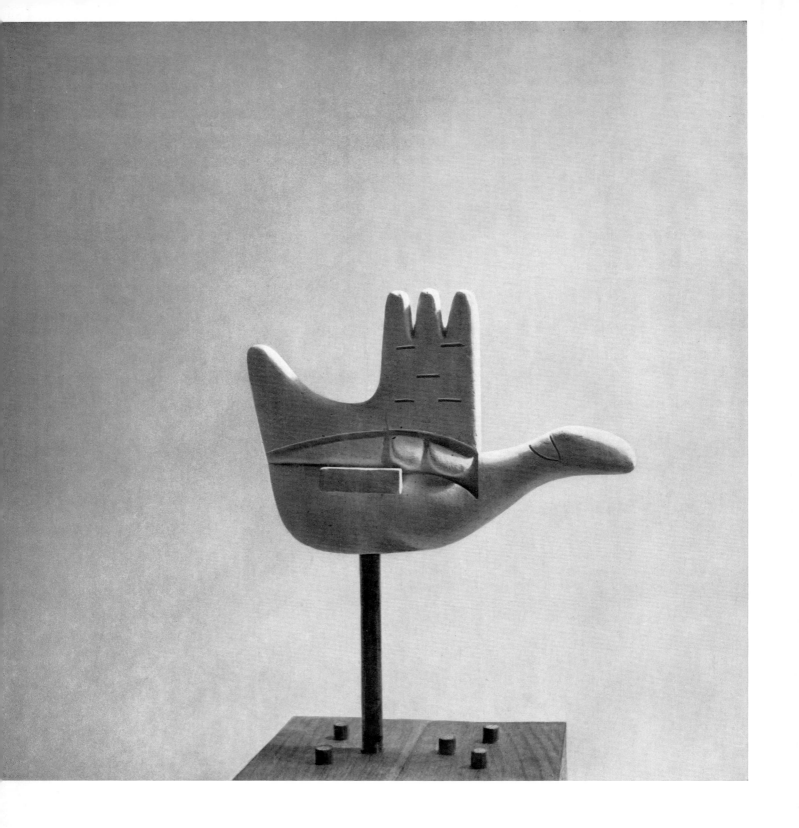

" *The Open-Hand*
to receive
and to give
at the moment where the modern world
is bursting into
infinite, unlimited richness
intellectual
and
material."

"The Open-Hand" which will spring nearly 100 feet out of the "Ditch of Consideration".

The High Court.

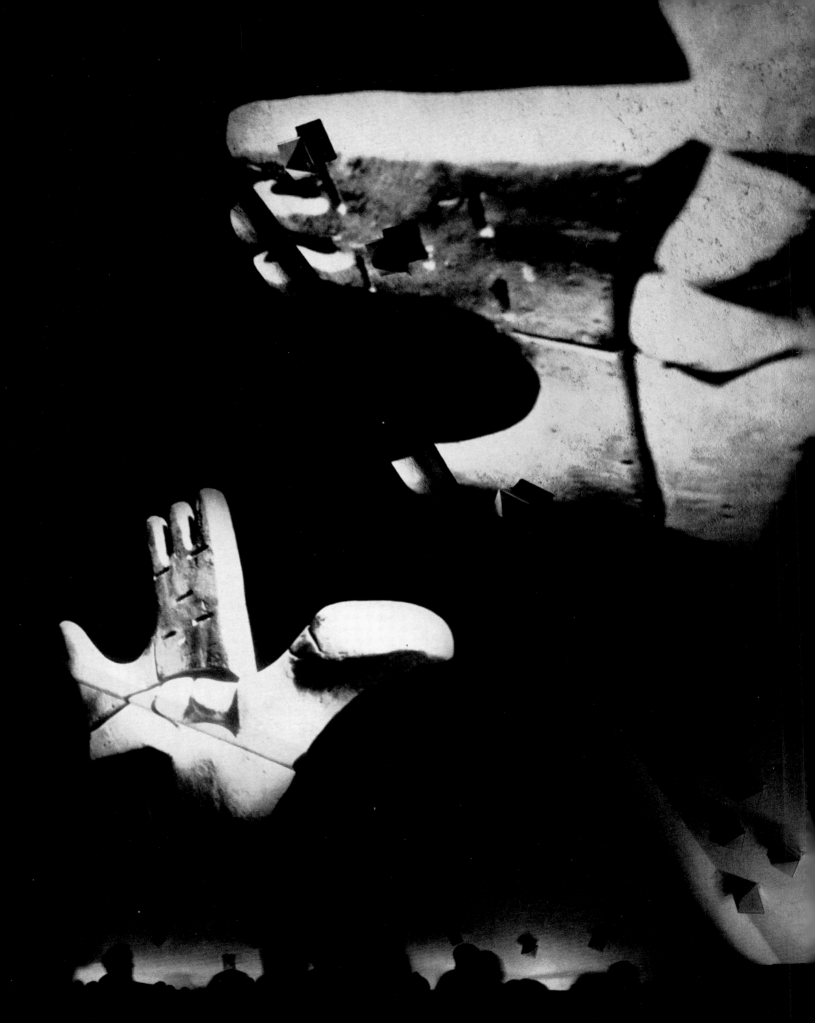

The Electronic Poem of the Philips Pavilion at the Brussels Exhibition 1958. Les Images.

Once again on the Marseilles roof: the infants' school. Did they know there was an Arcady like this, 200 feet up, with views in every direction? (See Page 293.)

Open air theatre on the Marseilles roof.

Chandigarh.

Sur les toits de Paris.

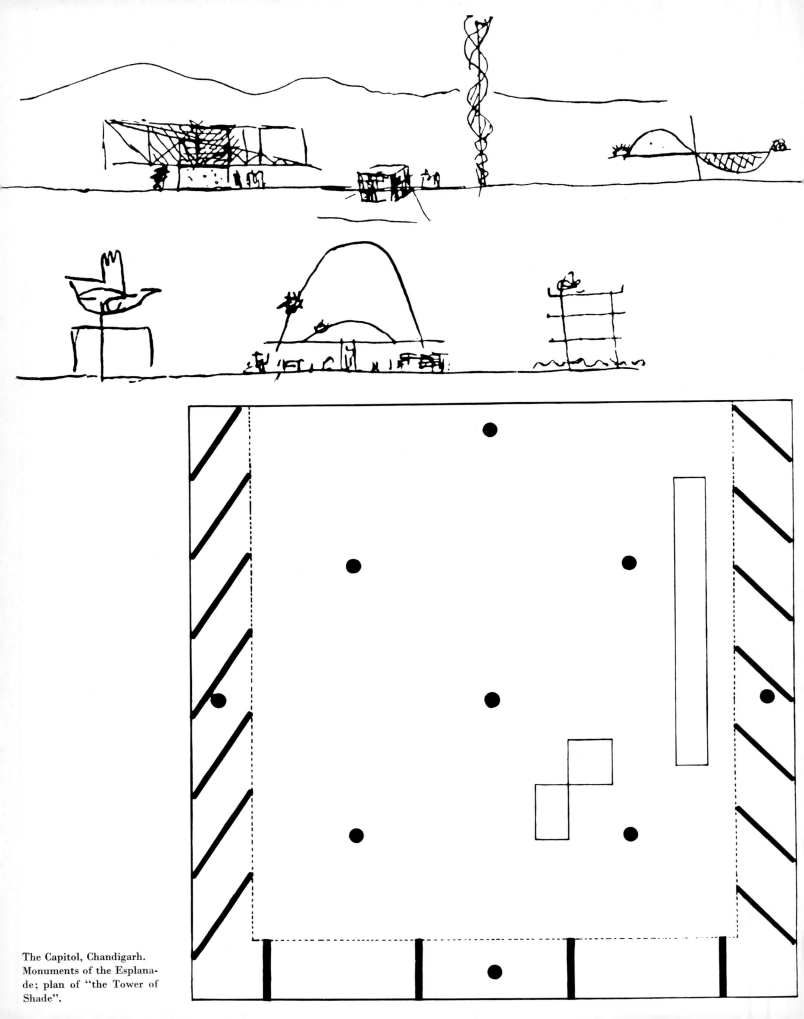

The Capitol, Chandigarh.
Monuments of the Esplana-
de; plan of "the Tower of
Shade".

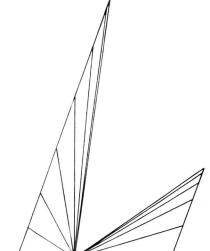

Sun-controls: page 289, model of the skyscraper at Algiers 1939;
pages 290 and 291, Chandigarh; on the right, the monument to
the course of the sun (Capitole).

1929. For Buenos Aires.

1929. For Montevideo and São Paulo.

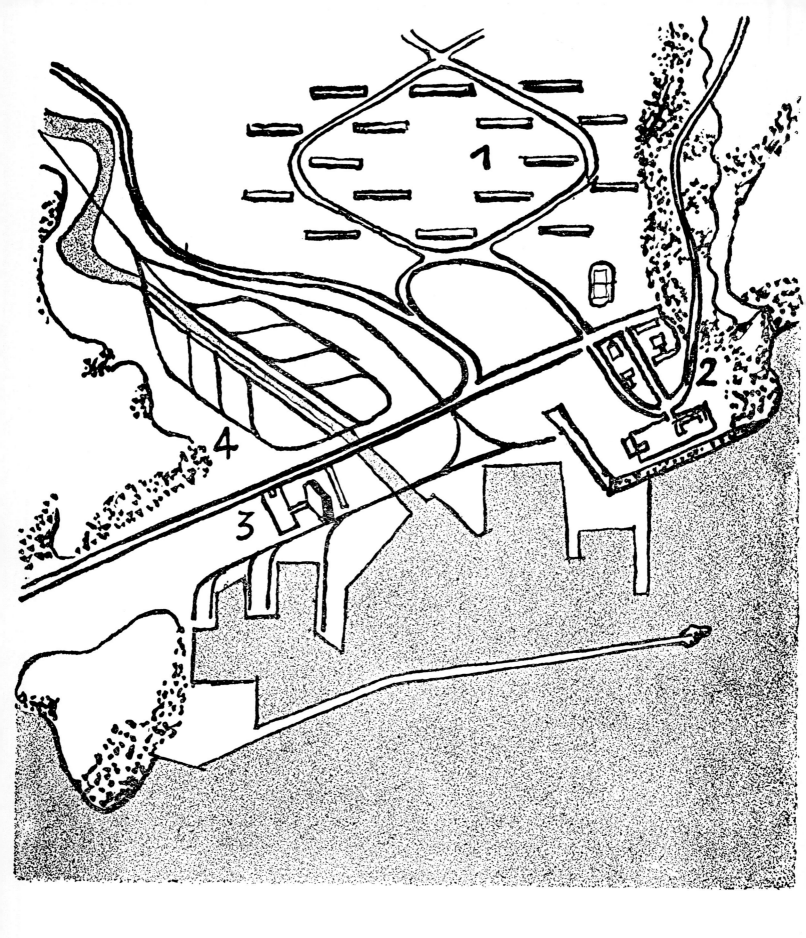

1934. For Nemours d'Afrique.

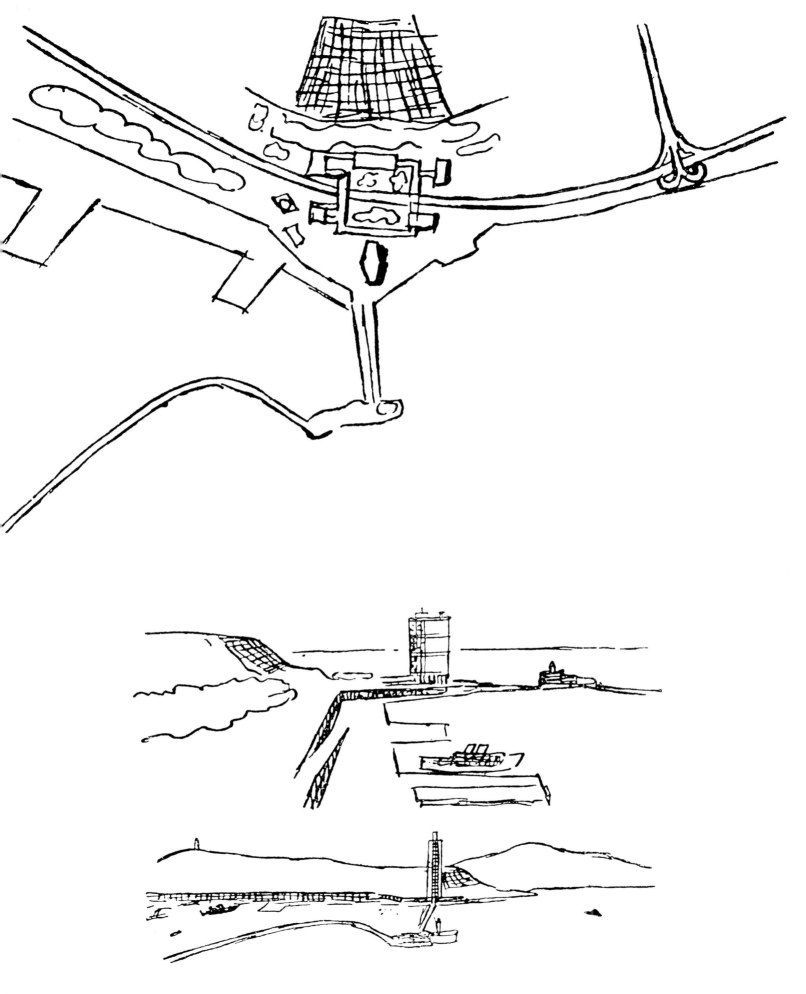

1939. For Algiers.

This is all topsy-turvy. The Parthenon is set on a plain, a hill or a mountain. Santa Maria del Fiore is on a plain, or in a fold of the hills or on top of an acropolis. The Gothic building is on a plain, on a hill or in a deep valley in the mountains. The modern block is also placed in three totally different settings. This proves that there is plenty of nonsense talked in learned expositions and that anything can be right, the only question being how rightly the thing is done.

OTHER TOOLS

Certain things have to be thought out in the abstract, to be debated in the mind or aloud, alone or in friendly (or unfriendly) discussion.

> To devise, to compose, to formulate and then to state....
> To state in writing or by the spoken word.

Much of what L-C has created has been worked out in his books on the one hand, and in his public statements on the other (all over the world, and beginning as far back as 1920 .... for forty years).

4 The written and the spoken word

BBC
Television (British Broadcasting)
émise le 15 mars 1959 à 20½ heures
(enregistrée dans l'appartement
de L-C à Paris le 27 janvier 1959

"*I am 71 years old.*

I have built my first house at the age of 17½ years and have continued during more than 50 years, occupied with many adventures and difficulties, catastrophes and from time to time success.

My research is, like my feelings, directed towards what is the principal value in the life: the poetry.

Poetry is in the heart of man and is the capacity to go into the richness of nature.

I am a visual man, a man working with eyes and hands, animated by plastic endeavour.

All that makes true architecture

> *true painting*
>
> *true planning for town and country.*

I have invented the word 'Ville-Radieuse', which cannot be translated in English perhaps, it is told to me!

But architecture and urbanism (or planning for town and country) are, in fact, one problem only and are not separate questions.

They demand one solution only and this is the work of one profession only.

My cities are green cities.

My houses give: sun

> *space*
>
> *and green.*

But to obtain such richness of life: sun, space and green, you must take 2,000 people together, build a big house with one entrance only for 2,000 people. So they will be quickly in their own home where they will find total silence and total solitude ... though they are 2,000 together. They will never hear them and never see them because it is possible to have one vertical road that is four rapid lifts (for 20 persons each), seven internal horizontal streets, one above the other, and four sets of neighbours: one above, two beside (left and right) and one below. That is the reason which brings to the modern man individual liberty and the benefit of communal resources.

The distances totally reduced and the traffic will be organized: the automobile will be separated from the pedestrians.

It lacks something:

the modern society, – very much occupied by its daily difficulties, has forgotten this:

> *one man*
>
> *one woman*
>
> *one child*
>
> *sleep in their bed;*
>
> *they awake, they go to their work*
>
> *then they come back to sleep in their bed.*

When such a state of affairs is brought to the attention, it will immediately be solved.

But this *problem is not brought before the attention of the authorities*
                              of the government
                              of the engineers
                              of the architects
                              of the people themselves.
And actually the millions and milliards of men, women and children of the world, each day are making a mad rush,
which is the terrific waste of modern life:
      they live where they should not live
      they work where they should not work.
The actual problem is to find again the conditions of nature.
And the answer is the major problem of to-day and to-morrow: the proper occupation *of the land, – that is the pro-*
per occupation of the globe, – which world is round and continuous!
And it is now this big task facing us: the occupation of the ground by human labor: "The three human estab-
lishments" *which are:*
      1. the Unity of Agricultural Exploitation
      2. the linear industrial city
      3. the radioconcentric town for trade, ideas, Government (that is exchange).
And please note that: since the beginning, there were only two Establishments :
      – agriculture and
      – exchange
      and nothing for industry, because industry did not exist.
The first *industrial era began a hundred years ago and it was an age of chaos.*
The second industrial era will be the era of harmony *and is only just beginning.*
The whole world is ready (open the eyes and the ears!) and all things are now fluid.
This is true, because the human scale is being considered afresh."

                                        Paris, 27th January 1959
                                        Le Corbusier

Après 50 années de voyages à travers le monde, je me sens le droit de dire que j'ai appris quelque chose, discerné des choses . . . . . . et même trouvé une solution. Lequel de mes négateurs sempiternels peut-il me contester ce droit?
Au terme de ce livre je puis dire que je suis effaré!!! J'ai mesuré que les hommes politiques et que les hommes de la politique sont demeurés, non pas indifférents, mais étrangers à l'urbanisme, — en dehors de l'urbanisme — L'URBANISME qui est l'expression de l'activité d'une époque. Et les POLITICIENS étant ceux dont le devoir est d'être les agents agissant d'une société !

BUT....

the academy says:

NO!

(Buenos Aires Lectures, 1929.)

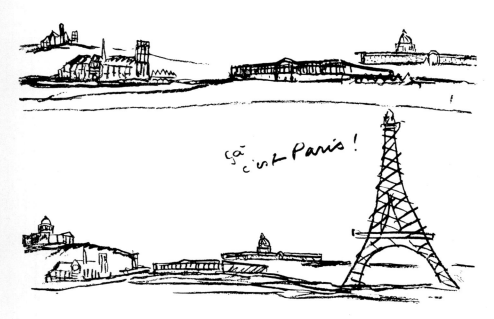

L'académisme dit: Non!

ee pages 171, 255,
*2, 273.

THEN, YOUTH AROSE ....

On 4th February 1960, four thousand five hundred young people thronged in front of the Sorbonne in Paris. Only three thousand could get into the large amphitheatre. Fifteen hundred filled the Rue des Ecoles up to the Boulevard St. Michel.

PARIS!

To that important centre of ideas, to the Sorbonne, came 3,000 members
of the Faculties of Medicine, Letters and Arts....

> *"Truth does not lie in extremes.*
> *It flows between two banks,*
> *A tiny, trickling, brook*
> *Or mighty flooding river,*
> *It differs every day!"*

"A book is now being printed, in several languages, on the research in which I have been engaged for more than fifty years. The final page of this book proposes a revolutionary issue: the sustained, patient and fruitful *conversation* between architect and engineer, engineer and architect, speaking as equals, with equal responsibilities and prestige. This conversation is that of the 'constructors'.

Nothing can now be constructed without this patient and profitable understanding between engineer and architect, each knowing his place, each recognising his duties and his rights.

Formerly, at the beginning of the machine age, the engineer was often timid and self-effacing. In contrast, the architect was often pompous, omniscient, trailing clouds of pretension. But things have changed! The tendency now is for the engineer to be scornful and agressive towards the architect enthroned above him. And so the fight is on! My theory (see sketch) will establish peace, and bring collaboration and efficiency to the aid of the 'constructors'.

During the Occupation, I founded the AS-CORAL, and I then tried to indicate, in a symbolical drawing, the differing responsibilities of the 'constructors' – the architects, the engineers – working alongside each other, but along different lines. In my drawing, of two spheres, I placed the sphere of the architect above that of the engineer.

In 1959, in the book mentioned above, I gave a quarter turn to my drawing, thus bringing architect and engineer together on a horizontal line – on the same level, but with differing tasks and responsibilities.

These then are the engineer's responsibilities: the respect of physical laws, the strength of materials (supply, economic considerations, etc. in relation to safety, relatively speaking).

And these the architect's: humanism, creative imagination, love of beauty, freedom of choice. In my drawing, the engineer's sphere casts a reflection on that of the architect – the reflection of the knowledge of physical laws. Similarly, the architect's understanding of human problems is reflected in the sphere of the engineer.

The shaded areas of the sketch indicate the world of the engineer, the dotted areas that of the architect. Under this symbolic composition I have placed two clasped hands, the fingers enlaced horizontally, demonstrating the friendly solidarity of both architect and engineer engaged, on the same level, in building the civilisation of the machine age. This is the emblem of the 'Constructors'."

Le Corbusier.

(Extract from "Science et Vie", August 1960.)

ASCORAL

Assemblée
de Constructeurs
pour une
Rénovation
Architecturale

The emblem of the ASCORAL. 1941. 306

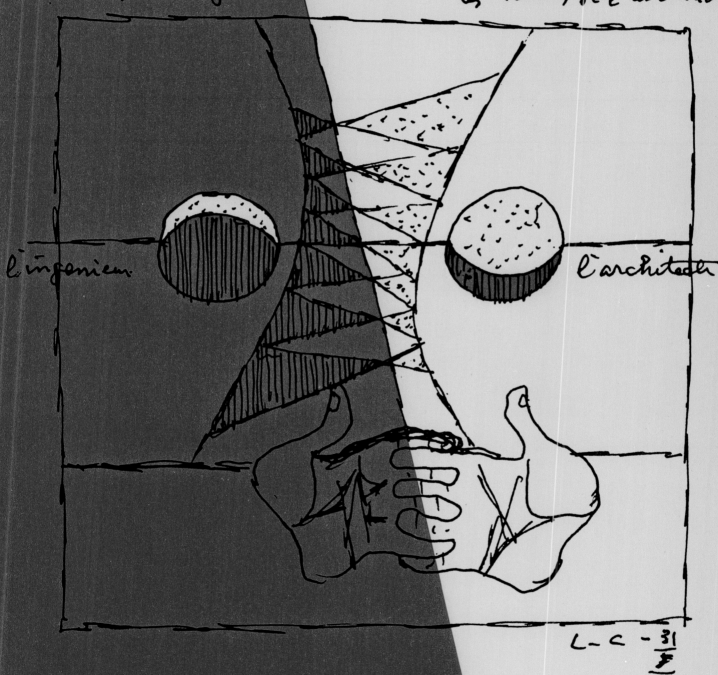

Les tâches de l'ingénieur

Les tâches de l'architecte

l'ingénieur

l'architecte

L-C - 31/X/60

Studio Le Corbusier 35 rue de Sèvres, Paris (since 1922). Thirty eight years ....

THANKS TO ALL!

Those who helped, 35 rue de Sèvres.... We worked in friendship, conviction and confidence.

The method of classifying did not begin until 28 February 1925, the numbers of the drawings, starting at 501, reaching 5635 on 19 November 1959.

Le Corbusier – Pierre Jeanneret – Emery – François Faure – 1925 – Roth – 1929 – Weismann – Frey – Mayekawa – Sert – Burhan – Sokol – Tsuchihashi – Rice – Wettstein – Busztin – Colley – 1930 – Beathy – Geiser – Saporta – Ducret – Size – Mme Perriand – Safranek – MacIver – Erlich – Renner – Michaelides – Komter – Weber – Vànec – Chavardes – Brechbühler – 1931 – Bossu – Alazard – Delporte – Senn – von Tobel – Oreste Maltos – Orazèm – Sedlak – André – MacCellan – Altherr – Wanner – Bosshardt – Jansen – Sakakura – Sammer – Poursain – David – Gruson – Stephenson – Kepes – 1932 – Joss – West – Waldkirch – Oswald – Davilla – White – Streiff – Streb – Adam – Castrillo – Feiniger – Cronstedt – 1933 – Diehl – Burckhardt – Neidhardt – Kropf – Verrier – Sever – Salomonson – Gomez Gavazzo – Reiner – Miquel – Berhamnc – 1934 – Barkaï – Boyer – Rentsch – 1935 – Pollak – Fawcett – Dupré – Hornstra – Schneider – 1936 – Braem – Mercier – Pantovic – Benes – 1937 – Christen – Dubois – 1938 – Krunic – Renard – Burri – 1939 – Tépina – Almairac – Ravnikar – Willem H. G. de Moor – Epio Borg – Wogenscky – Nielsen Tage – Hanning – 1940 – Welti – Zupo – Pfister – Zupencic – Bollinger – de Graaf – 1944 – Aujame – de Looze – 1945 – Soltan – 1946 – Bodiansky – Danielle Janin – Candilis – Gardien – Zalewsky – Dubois – 1947 – Nadir Afonso – Michaud – Andréini – 1948 – Gonzales de Léon – Masson – Salmona – Weismann – Pirko Hirvela – 1949 – Bruaux – Kennedy – Provelenghios – Vaculic – Woods – Hoesli – Olek Kujawski – Xénakis – Clémot – Samper – Serralta – Solomita – Wurster – Takamasa Yosizaka – Walter – Valencia – Mme Heilbuth – 1951 – Maisonnier – Mazet – Doshi – Pérez – 1952 – Michel – Lemarchand – Mériot – Duhart – Kim Chun Up – Melle Gabillard – 1953 – Véret – Tobito – Sachinidis – 1954 – Talati – 1959 – Jullian – Tavés – Oubrerie.

Xénakis, Maisonnier, Tobito, who left the studio in 1959, asked to be called: architectes chefs d'études.

5 Those who helped

BIBLIOGRAPHY

ETUDE DU MOUVEMENT D'ART
DECORATIF EN ALLEMAGNE
1911

APRES LE CUBISME (avec Ozenfant)
1918

VERS UNE ARCHITECTURE
(Collection de l'Esprit Nouveau)
1923

LA PEINTURE MODERNE
(avec Ozenfant)
1925

L'ART DECORATIF D'AUJOURD'HUI
(Collection de l'Esprit Nouveau)
1925

URBANISME
(Collection de l'Esprit Nouveau)
1925

ALMANACH DE L'ARCHITECTURE
MODERNE
(Collection de l'Esprit Nouveau)
1927

UNE MAISON – UN PALAIS
(Collection de l'Esprit Nouveau)
1928

PRECISIONS SUR UN ETAT PRE-
SENT DE L'ARCHITECTURE ET
L'URBANISME
(Collection de l'Esprit Nouveau)
1930

CROISADE – Le Crépuscule des
Académies
(Collection de l'Esprit Nouveau)
1932

LA VILLE-RADIEUSE
(Collection de l'Equipement de la
Civilisation machiniste)
1935

AIRCRAFT
(Collection The New Vision)
1935

QUAND LES CATHEDRALES
ETAIENT BLANCHES
Voyage aux pays des timides
1937

DES CANONS, DES MUNITIONS?
MERCI! DES LOGIS... S.V.P.
(Collection de l'Equipement de la
Civilisation machiniste)
1938

LE LYRISME DES TEMPS NOUVEAUX
ET L'URBANISME
1939

DESTIN DE PARIS
1941

SUR LES 4 ROUTES
1941

LA MAISON DES HOMMES
(avec François de Pierrefeu)
1942

PROPOS D'URBANISME
1945

UNE PETITE MAISON
(Carnet de la recherche patiente)
1954

LES CONSTRUCTIONS
MURONDINS
1941

U.N. HEADQUARTERS
1947

LE MODULOR 2
1955

LA CHARTE D'ATHENES
(avec un Discours Liminaire de Jean
Giraudoux)
1943

NEW WORLD OF SPACE
1948

LE POEME DE L'ANGLE DROIT
1955

ENTRETIEN AVEC LES ETUDIANTS
DES ECOLES D'ARCHITECTURE
1943

LE MODULOR
1949

LES PLANS LE CORBUSIER DE
PARIS 1953–1922
1956

LES TROIS ETABLISSEMENTS
HUMAINS
(Collection Ascoral)
1945

POESIE SUR ALGER
1950

RONCHAMP
(Carnet de la recherche patiente)
1957

MANIERE DE PENSER
L'URBANISME
(Collection Ascoral)
1945

L'UNITE D'HABITATION DE
MARSEILLE
1950

LE CORBUSIER
1960